God's Chosen People: Abraham to Christ

john E. filippi

Search for the Truth Publications
3275 Monroe Rd.
Midland, MI 48642
989.837.5546
www.searchforthetruth.net

Published by:
Search for the Truth Publications
www.searchforthetruth.net

Foreword

The Word of God is a profound mystery unless you understand how it originated. Written by 40 authors over a 3500 year period it tells a unified story of mankind's sad history of rebellion against our Creator. Yet it is also the glorious account of our merciful Creator's desire and method for drawing us back into fellowship with Him. The Bible repeatedly verifies its true authorship by telling the future in advance with specific detailed accuracy. Only the Creator of the universe (who is therefore outside of our physical and material universe…and thus outside of time as we know it) could accomplish such a feat. Most churches concentrate upon the central focus of human history – Jesus…God coming as man…Emmanuel…God with flesh on! Yet this act of redemption cannot be properly understood without the background of the Old Testament. *God's Chosen People* is John Filippi's humble attempt to make the greatest book of truth and knowledge ever penned accessible and understandable to those who have not submersed themselves within its unfathomable depth.

Far too many people spend their waning years on pursuits of no eternal value. John Filippi has chosen to spend his time authoring a book whose purpose is introducing future generations to the treasure of God's Word. After over eight decades upon the earth, John is more passionate than ever about the scope of God's love and the accuracy of God's Word. May I be so faithful if blessed with as many years to serve the Lord!

No human book can compare to reading, studying, and meditating upon the Word of God. But if this volume motivates even one person to do so, the cost and effort has been worthwhile. I am proud to call John Filippi my friend and contribute in a small way to his work.

Bruce Malone
Editor and Christian brother

Acknowledgements

This book draws heavily from insights found in the *New Defender's Study Bible* (King James Version) with the annotations prepared by Henry M. Morris, Ph.D., LL.D. I refer heavily upon his introductions to the various books of the Bible as well as the explanatory notations from some of the Bible verses. I highly recommend this Bible for those desiring to increase their knowledge of God's Word.

In my first book *By His Word*, I used (with permission) Grant R. Jeffrey's *The Mysterious Bible* Codes pages 184-187. In this book, I have used information from Jeffrey's new book, *Countdown to the Apocalypse*, being certain to credit the appropriate page. If you desire to know more details of the end times, I highly recommend *Countdown to the Apocalypse*.

Dedication

This book is dedicated to my Christian brother Bruce Malone who edited and published the manuscript. I am deeply indebted to Bruce for the arrangement and flow of my words. Bruce is the executive director of Search for the Truth Ministries in Midland, Michigan. This book is also dedicated to two other Christian brother, Christopher Greaves of Rainbow Springs Village Church in Dunnellon, Florida, and to Michael Carriere of Evergreen Christian Church, Negaunee, Michigan who are shephards and teach God's word as it is written! I am also indebted to my sister Pearl Filizetti for making the final corrections.

Preface

I was baptized and confirmed in the Finnish Evangelical Lutheran Church in the upper peninsula of Michigan. Moving to Lansing, Michigan in 1947, I joined the Augustana Lutheran Church (this was a Swedish branch and one-quarter of my heritage is Swedish). In 1962, both churches joined the

Lutheran Church in America (LCA). In 1988, another merger took place and the churches joined forming the Evangelical Lutheran Church in America (ELCA).

Since 1991, I have been actively studying about Biblical creation through Duane T. Gish, Ph.D. who introduced me to the works of Henry M. Morris and The Institute for Creation Research. From this affiliation, I became associated with Ken Ham and the Answers in Genesis team. After years of study, God gave me the desire to develop a creation evangelism program.

Since that time, I have tried to teach Biblical creation in our Evangelical Lutheran Church in America with very sad results. When approached, most churches and their leadership want little to do with teaching the Bible as God's authoritative word in a straightforward understandable way. Finally, in September of 2008, God made it clear that it was time to move to more fertile ground.

I found one piece of fertile ground with Rainbow Springs Village Church, affiliated with Christian Missionary Alliance, in Dunnellon, Florida. My wife Vivian (also friend and Christian sister) and I became members on Palm Sunday April 5, 2009. We are also members of Evergreen Christian Church of Negaunee, Michigan in the Upper Peninsula. This is a non-denominational Bible believing church we helped Pastor Michael Carriere organize on September 17, 2007.

I am now over eighty years old and my desire to serve the Lord grows stronger each year. Over the last decade, I have seen many people's foundation of faith eroded and destroyed because they have accepted the lie that the Bible cannot be believed as written. This is especially true of Genesis and the early books of the Bible. Thus evangelism of our nation must begin by re-establishing the trust in God's Word beginning with creation in Genesis. This is creation evangelism. Only our Lord knows where He will take me with my creation evangelism program. Daily I work so that I may have something worthwhile to offer at His feet at the day of my accounting. I praise the Lord every day he gives me for this opportunity.

John E. Filippi

Introduction

My previous book, *BY HIS WORD: A Wakeup Call to America's Churches*, presented Creation Evangelism and covered the seven C's of biblical history:

1. Creation - where everything came from
2. Corruption - why death, disease, and problems exist
3. Catastrophe - the reality of a world wide flood
4. Confusion - why people groups and nations (not races) exist
5. Christ - God entering into human history
6. Cross – Jesus, His act of love, taking the death penalty we deserve upon Himself
7. Consummation – restoration and the wrapping up of history

The first four C's cover almost 2000 years of earth history yet the Bible covers this same period of earth history in a mere eleven chapters in Genesis. *By His Word* was largely silent on the later history of the Bible. Everything which happened from Abraham to Christ, including the development of three major world religions (all proclaiming Abraham as the father) was only mentioned briefly in *By His Word*. Therefore, this sequel begins in Genesis 12 with the introduction of Abraham. This book is a very brief overview of the history of humanity from the time of Abraham to Christ. It is a humbling task to even begin to try and summarize all of the depth and breath of knowledge and spiritual lessons contained within God's Word. But it is my hope that this humble overview will familiarize the reader with a few key concepts from the Bible which show how God's sovereign hand has guided human history. In many cases, especially in the later books of the Old Testament, very little of the text will be discussed. The reader is encouraged to read God's Word for himself rather than just my summary. I merely give you an overview of the setting and purpose for each book.

Looking back to Genesis 11, we find the history of humanity from the first man Adam leading all the way to the

Messiah. This family line moved through one unique man by the name of Abraham, the oldest son of Terah. At that time, his name is not Abraham but Abram. We also learn that Abram is married to a woman named Sarai who is barren (having no children). Interestingly, Abram's wife, Sarai is also Abram's half sister. This marriage of close relations is not possible today because of the rapid build up of genetic mistakes upon the human genome. Even if marriage of siblings was allowed legally today, these unions would not be wise. Now children from closely related parents are prone to major genetic defects and health problems. However, a mere 4000 years ago such unions were allowed and common because there were not many genetic mistakes in the human DNA code. This is one of many strong evidences that the human race was created quite recently, just as the Bible states.

Abram's father Terah took Abram and Sarai as well as Lot(Abram's nephew) from Ur of the Chaldeans into the land of Canaan. They came unto Haran and dwelt there, where Terah died at the age of 205 years. Although such longevity is unheard of today, the superior genetic make-up of early humans is quite likely the reason they lived much longer. In spite of phenomenal advances in medical science, the average lifetime of a man in the Western world today (82 years) is scarcely more than that at the time of King David over 2000 years ago (Psalm 90:10 states that the life of man is 70-80 years). Yet, at the time Genesis 1-12 was written (approximately 4000 years ago), it was common for people to live 200 years or more. Obviously there has been a rapid deterioration of our DNA structure which prevents such long lives. The world that now exists is also a more hostile environment than the original paradise which existed on the earth before the worldwide flood. Hebrew states that the existing world was deluged and destroyed. The world before the flood was totally different in topography and climate than anything we experience today. Once again, this is an indication that things have changed radically here on earth in known historical times and that people have not been around for millions of years.

Throughout this book, I will refer to God as our "triune God". I do this to emphasize that the God we worship is not the same God as the Hindu's, Muslim's, New Age believers or any other world religion. The Creator God is one God yet three distinct persons. We have God the Father who is over all creation. Secondly, we have God the Son who made all of creation and who became a human being to take the sin penalty we deserve (yet could never pay). Thirdly, we have God the Spirit who draws us to himself, reveals our sinful nature, and lives within us once we accept Jesus' sacrifice. All are God; yet all are distinct. Although this mystery will not be fully understood until we are with Him in heaven, I will use the term "triune God."

I have also attempted to tell the story of God's redemption of mankind (return to fellowship) though the use of many direct quotes and narratives from the Bible. Direct quotes from God's Word are placed in italics throughout the book.

Table of Contents

part 1

Genesis 12 to 36
The Patriarchs: Abraham, Isaac, & Jacob

Genesis 12

Chapter 12 of Genesis shifts gear and the narrative slows down as God begins a relationship with a select group of people by making a covenant (solemn unconditional promise) with Abram. God tells Abram to leave his father's house and go to a land which would be given to him and his descendants. Abram (75 years of age at this time), Sarai, and Lot did not go directly to the Promised Land. They left Haran and went to Sichem unto the plain of Moreh, in the land of Canaan, which was occupied by the Canaanites. In a theophany (an Old Testament appearance of Jesus), the Lord appeared unto Abram and said, "Unto thy seed will I give this land." Abram built an altar to worship God upon this significant spot. He also built a second altar unto the Lord between Bethel and Hai where he called upon the name of the Lord. Abram was learning to trust the Lord but still relied on himself as much as God's sovereignty. Yet the Lord told Abram that he would become a great nation, his name would be great, he would be a blessing to all, the Lord would bless those who bless him and curse those who curse him.

Because of famine, Abram and Sarai went into Egypt where Abram "half-lied" to the Pharaoh about Sarai's true relation to him. Apparently, Sarai was a remarkably beautiful lady and Abraham, fearing for his life, told Pharaoh that Sarai was his sister. She was taken into Pharaoh's court. Even in this early culture, adultery was recognized as a sin and Pharaoh was extremely displeased when he learned Abram had not told him that Saral was his wife. The Pharaoh reprimanded Abram and sent him and Sarai away with all their property. Abram was learning to totally trust God. If God had allowed the famine, then he was capable of taking care of Abram without his manipulation of circumstances with lies and deceit. Yet Abram's actions showed he did not yet understand this truth.

Genesis 13

This chapter covers the separation of Abram from Lot. God had blessed Abram so that he became very rich with large herds and possessions. Lot had also been blessed and became very prosperous. As a result, Abram's and Lot's servants and herdsmen fought. Since they were closely related, Abram and Lot went before the Lord and prayed at the second altar that there would be no strife between them. They agreed to separate with Lot selecting the plain of Jordan where he pitched his tent near the city of Sodom. It is stated here that the men of Sodom were wicked and sinners, exceedingly, before the Lord. Apparently later Lot moved into this very wicked town. (There is a spiritual lesson here -we cannot toy with or live near evil, without having evil draw us closer and affect our lives.)

Abram continued to dwell in the land of Canaan. God promised Abram that he would give him and his seed all of the land which he could see to the North, South, East, and West. The Lord also said that Abraham's seed will be like the dust of the Earth,too numerous to count. The Lord told Abram to walk the length and breadth of the land for it is yours. So Abram moved his tent and dwelt in the plain of Mamre, in Hebron, where he built the third altar unto the Lord.

Genesis 14

Abram has to rescue Lot for the first time (God rescues him a second time in Chapter 19). War had been raged against Bera (King of Sodom) and Birsha (King of Gomorrah). At this time in earth history, kingdoms often consisted of one small town. King's Chedorlaomer, King Tidal, King Amraphel, and King Arioch joined to defeat the Kings of Sodom and Gomorrah. All the people and goods of Sodom and Gomorrah including Lot and his possessions were taken. Abram heard that Lot was captive so he armed his 318 trained servants (essentially a private army) and pursued them unto Dan. By dividing his forces and attacking at night, Abram and his men conquered the four kingdoms and pushed them all the way back into Hobah. Abram brought Lot and his family home with all of the plundered goods.

This is where we learn of Melchizedek, the King of Salem. In the Old Testament, the names of people often have great sig-

Abraham Meets Melchizedek

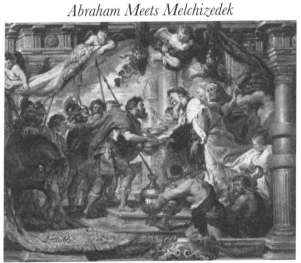

Peter Paul Rubens - ca. 1625

nificance. Melchizedek means king of righteousness and salem means peace. David called Melchizedek "the Lord, a priest forever". Taken literally, these words would only be applicable to Christ himself. Whenever God appears before people in the Old Testament, it is called a theophany. Abram gave a tithe (one tenth of his gains) to Melchizedek. Since the tithe is meant for the Lord, this is further evidence that the Lord appeared to Abram.

Upon returning from defeating the four kingdoms, the king of Sodom told Abram to keep the goods but return the people to me. Abram said that he would accept nothing lest he be accused of making himself rich at the king's expense. Abram was showing himself to be a man of integrity who trusted God more than riches. Abram only asked for the food his men had eaten and that Aner, Eshcol and Mamre take their portions.

Genesis 15

In this chapter, God promised Abram an heir. Abram believed in the Lord and he counted that faith as righteousness. This is the first mention of belief or faith in the Bible. Faith in this case emphasized the divine side and the phrase "counted it to him" emphasized the human side.

God also promised Abram's seed all the land from the river of Egypt to the Euphrates River. Abram asked the Lord God, "How shall I know that I shall inherit this land?" The Lord told him to prepare a sacrifice which was the customary procedure at the time in establishing a solemn compact. The sacrifice was cut in half. Then the contracting parties sealed the covenant by passing between the two halves of the slaughtered animal. However, only God passed through since the covenant was a unilateral, unconditional commitment on His part. God told Abram that his seed would be a stranger in a land that is not theirs and that they would become slaves for four hundred years. Later those who afflicted Abram's descendants would come under God's judgment and Abram's people would receive great wealth. This is an exact prediction of the future events which took place in Egypt. Throughout scripture, God predicts the future to validate that the Bible is indeed inspired and written by Him.

Genesis 16

We encounter Abram making his own plan to have children in Chapter 16. Many years have passed without an heir being born, so Abram and Sarai decided to take things into their own hands. Abram demonstrated that he did not yet fully trust the Lord. Since Sarai bore Abram no children, she proposed a plan for Abram to have a child with her maid Hagar. This was a common practice in that culture. Abram had sex with Sarai's servant and she conceived. However, Sarai became jealous of Hagar and treated her so harshly that Hagar fled from the household. The Lord spoke to Hagar by a fountain of water in the wilderness (either audibly or spiritually). Hagar explained to the Lord why she was running away. The Lord told Hagar to return and submit to Sarai and to name her son Ishmael. However, God also predicted that Ishmael would be a wild man with a life of conflict and that he would dwell in the presence of his brethren. God repeatedly predicts the future and exactly what He has predicted ALWAYS becomes precisely true. God the Creator is actually outside of time and sees all of eternity, the past, the present, and the future simultaneously. This is one of the many ways we can know that the Bible is actually the word of God and not just a book written by man. Thus Hagar bore a son and named him Ishmael

Chapter 16 has the first use of term, "the angel of the Lord". This seems to refer to Christ himself. Many Biblical scholars believe this is another example of Jesus appearing upon the earth to interact with humanity thousands of years in advance of God becoming human at the time of Christ's birth. In other words, we have yet another theophany (the appearance of God to His people).

Genesis 17

This chapter covers the covenant of circumcision. The Lord came to Abram again and he fell on his face and God said, *"You will be a father of many nations."* God went on to state that Abram's name would be changed to Abraham (the father of many nations). This covenant God made with Abraham was for all his descendants and was testified to by the act of circumcision. Circumcision was done on the eighth day after birth (which turns out to be the optimum time for a baby's blood to clot properly). Abraham was told to do this for all his household and that those who were not circumcised would be cut off because they have broken God's covenant. This was a serious non-negotiable commitment to follow the Lord and those who were not circumcised would have no fellowship with God.

At this same time, Sarai's name was changed to Sarah. This change of name is a symbol of our change in nature when we truly commit to following the Lord. God promised to bless her and to make her the mother of nations. It is extremely significant that Abraham and Sarah were to be a blessing to ALL nations, not just the nation of Israel. God desires to draw all people from all nations to himself. Missions and evangelism is always central to God's purpose. When God promised that Sarah would have a child, Abraham fell on his face and laughingly said, *"Shall a child be born unto him that is 100 years old? Will Sarah bear a child at age ninety?"* Abraham then proposed, *"O that Ishmael might live before thee!"*

But God's plans are always better than our feeble attempts to work things out in our own strength. God responded, *"Sarah thy wife shall bear a son indeed; and thou shall call his name Isaac; and I will establish my covenant with him for an everlasting covenant and with his seed after him. As for Ishmael, I have heard your request and I will bless him and will make him fruitful, and will multiply him exceedingly; twelve princes shall he beget and I will make him a great nation. However, I will establish my covenant with Isaac which your wife Sarah will bear thee at this set time in the next year."* God then left and Abraham must have been in a state of shock and wonder. Abraham then took Ishmael his son and all of the other males in his household and they were circumcised just as God had commanded. Abraham was age 99 years and Ishmael was 13 years of age at the time of circumcision.

Genesis 18

The faith of Sarah was tested next. In the plain of Mamre, the Lord again appeared to Abraham as three visiting strangers. One of these strangers seems to be the Lord Jesus Christ and the other two, angels of the Lord. I believe them to be archangles Michael and Gabriel. The three of them ate the meat prepared by Sarah. After eating, two of the angels moved on to save

Abraham's nephew Lot who was living in the extremely wicked city of Sodom.

The Lord stayed with Abraham and asked, *"Where is Sarah thy wife?"* The Lord knows all things but often asks us questions for our benefit and clarification.

Abraham answered, *"Behold, in the tent."*

The Lord then responded, *"Sarah your wife shall have a son."*

God and the Angels visit Abraham

Arent de Gelder - c. 1680-1685

Overhearing this, Sarah laughed within herself knowing that she was too old to conceive. The Lord asked Abraham, *"Why did Sarah think she would not bear children since she was old? Is anything too hard for the Lord?"* This is perhaps one of the most encouraging truths of Scripture. It is reality that God exists outside of His creation and is in control of all creation – both in the past, present, and future. This gives us confidence that no matter what our situation, God reigns. He often works through natural circumstances but God is capable of supernatural intervention. Is anything too hard for the Lord? NO. With God all things are possible! The Lord goes on to promise, *"I will return to you at the appointed time and Sarah shall have a son."* Sarah denied laughing because she was afraid. But the Lord said, *"Yes, but you did laugh."*

In spite of Sarah's lack of faith, God did not reject Sarah but proceeded with his plan to give Abraham and Sarah an heir. It is through the heir's blood line that God Himself would someday become human.

This chapter also exemplifies the power of intercession before the Lord. Abraham questioned the Lord about destroying the righteous along with the wicked and then proceeded to ask the Lord to spare the city if even a few righteous are present. The Lord agreed to these requests (even though in reality none of us deserve this mercy because no human is truly righteous before the perfect holiness of the Lord). It is interesting that Abraham started with fifty but stops with ten. Ten is the number of relatives Abraham had in the city - Lot and his wife, their two sons (Genesis 19:12), two married daughters and their husbands (Genesis 19:8), and two unmarried daughters (Genesis 19:8). If ten righteous could be found, the Lord agreed to not destroy the city.

Genesis 19

The scene now shifts to the wicked city of Sodom. The two angels, appearing as ordinary people, show up in town to warn Lot to leave before judgment is brought upon the city. To this day, the term sodom is associated with homosexuality and perversion. Lot tried to keep the wicked men of Sodom from harming the two visitors. He even offered his own daughters for sexual molestation to the men surrounding his home in place of his two visitors. His home was surrounded by all the people of the town, both young and old. But God intervened and the crowd was struck blind. In the morning, the two angels instructed Lot to take his entire family out of the city prior to its destruction. Lot, his wife, and two daughters escaped from Sodom. His married daughters and two sons apparently declined to leave. Lot's wife looked back and became a pillar of salt. The language of this verse may also be interpreted that she lingered or held back and the phrase "turned to salt" could be explained as covered with ash and petrified.

Escaping total destruction of the city, Lot and his two daughters entered Zoar. Lot had children with his own daughters which resulted in two different Middle Eastern peoples. One named Moab whose followers were Moabites; the other named Benammi with Ammon followers. There is no mention of birth defect or problems which would have resulted from such unions today. Again, this is only possible because the DNA of early humans did not have the number of mistakes that are in human DNA today. This strongly indicates that humans have not been around for millions of years.

Abraham arose early that morning and stood in the place where he had met with the Lord. He looked toward Sodom and Gomorrah and saw rising smoke like the smoke of a furnace. God had heard Abraham's prayer and had rescued Lot from destruction.

Genesis 20

Abraham and Sarah journeyed to Gerar, a prosperous Philistine settlement along the coast near the Egyptian border. Abimelech, the king of Gerar, saw Sarah's beauty. For the second time, Abraham lied because he feared he would be killed if the king knew Sarah was his wife. Note that any statement made with the intent to deceive or hide the truth is a lie. There is no such thing as a half-truth, partial lie, or white lie. Lies always destroy trust and ultimately have negative consequences.

God came to Abimelech in a dream and said, *"Sarah, the woman you have taken, is a man's wife. Yes, I know that you did this in the integrity of your heart and so I have kept you from sinning against me. That is why I did not let you touch her. Now you must restore the man his wife for he is a prophet."* This is the first time the word prophet or prophecy is used in scripture. Abimelech returned Sarah to Abraham along with sheep, oxen, menservants, and maidservants and allowed Abraham to live in his land. Then Abraham prayed to God and God healed Abimelech, his wife and maidservants so they could bear children, since God had closed their wombs because of Sarah, Abraham's wife.

Genesis 21

This chapter covers the birth of Isaac. When Isaac was born, Abraham was 100 years old and Sarah was 90 years old. Isaac's birth brought laughter to Sarah. As previously stated, with God all things are possible. God instructed that Isaac be circumcised on the eighth day. Eight days old is important; coagulation (the thickening ability) of the blood is at its peak. Upon Isaac's weaning, Abraham held a great feast for his entire household. It may have been at this time that Sarah thought that Ishmael was mocking his half-brother. Ishmael was approximately 14 years old at the time. Sarah ordered Abraham to cast out this bondswomen and her son so that Ishmael would

Abraham Casting Out Hagar and Ishmael

Il Guercino - 1657

not be a joint heir with Isaac. Abraham was greatly distressed by Sarah's order. But God told Abraham that a great nation would come from Ishmael. Had Abraham kept Ishmael in his household, I believe Christianity would be worldwide. I believe Ishmael's followers would not be Islamic but Christians. Sadly, Abraham rose up early, took bread, a bottle of wine and gave it to Hagar (putting it on her shoulder in a carrying container) and sent her and Ishmael on their way. She departed and wandered in the wilderness called Beersheba. When her water and food were gone, Hagar laid Ishmael underneath a shrub and went away so she would not see him die. God heard Ishmael sobbing and said to Hagar, *"Arise, lift up the lad and hold him in your hand; for I will make him a great nation."* God provided water for them to drink. God was with Ishmael and he became an archer. He dwelt in the wilderness of Paran and Hagar selected a wife for him from Egypt.

At this point, the narrative returns to Abraham who was living in the land of the Philistines. Abimelech understood that Abraham was a prophet because God had answered Abraham's prayer (that the wombs of Abimelech's wives be opened). Abimelech requested that Abraham treat him, his children, and all his descendents with the same kindness that he had treated Abraham and his household. Abraham swore to Abimelech that he would reciprocate that kindness. They settled their differences over a well of water. Abraham gave Abimelech seven ewe lambs as a witness that Abraham had dug the well. Abraham dwelled in peace with the Philistines for many years. Abraham and Abimelech had made a covenant to each other. Although Abraham had made a covenant with a temporal king, he knew that he was the recipient of a covenant with an eternal king, our triune God. He planted a grove in Beersheba to the everlasting God.

Genesis 22

God tested (I use tested, from the Hebrew word nacah which translates proved, rather than tempted) Abraham's faith by asking him to offer Isaac as a sacrifice. Since this was a test of faith, God knew all along the outcome and had no intention of allowing Isaac to die. If Isaac had actually died, I suspect he would have been brought back to life. God had already promised Abraham that a great nation would come from Isaac. No doubt Abraham believed the same thing.

Why would God test Abraham in this way? In the past, Abraham had proven to be unfaithful by not believing God's word. This resulted in lies about Sarah and the birth of Ishmael (through whom countless future problems and conflicts would arise). God needed Abraham to understand that nothing should

The Sacrifice of Isaac

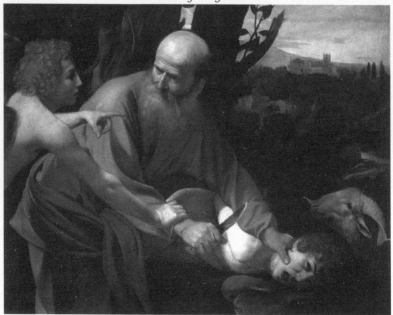

Caravaggio - ca. 1603

stand between his faith and total obedience to the Lord. Not even his love for his own son. Abraham proved his faithfulness by preparing Isaac as a sacrifice.

Isaac was old enough to know that it was a Canaanite practice to sacrifice their first born son to their god. Isaac was also strong enough to escape if he desired to do so. Isaac questioned, *"Where is the lamb for the burnt offering?"* Abraham's answered only, *"God will provide."* Still, they went on together. Abraham must have instilled in his son the same kind of faith. It took Abraham three days to travel to the place of sacrifice, the same amount of time of our Lord's burial. The sacrifice location was Mount Moriah, the place where Christ would one day offer himself as the lamb of God. Is there any doubt that this incident between Abraham and Isaac was a preview of the agony that God the Father would go through when he sent his son to die for us? If we believe in Him, our sins are forgiven and we will inherit His Kingdom. Just as Abraham offered his only son as a sacrifice, so God sacrificed his only son for us. We have a God of incomprehensible love!

When God saw that Abraham feared Him to the point of sacrificing Isaac, God provided a substitute (a ram) so that Isaac did not have to die - just as we have been provided a substitute (Jesus) so that we do not have to suffer eternal death and separation from God. God was laying a pattern of what was to come. Abraham named this place, Jehovah Jireh, which means God provides. Because Abraham did not withhold his son, his **only** son, God promised again to bless ALL NATIONS through Abraham's offspring. The ultimate blessing, the means for humans to come back into fellowship with God (Jesus Christ), would come through the family line of Abraham. Notice that even though Abraham had two sons, it was only Isaac, the son provided by God, who was considered a son. What we do on our own strength has no value to the Lord whereas what we do with the Lord's help has eternal consequences.

Genesis 23

Sarah died at the age of 127 years. Isaac was 37 years old at her death. Abraham sought a burial place for Sarah in Hebron in the land of Canaan. Abraham chose a cave of Machpelah which was in a field owned by Ephron. Although the property was worth four hundred shekels of silver, Ephron wanted to give Abraham the field and the cave. Ephron stated, *"What is this amount between you and I, just take it and bury your dead."* However, Abraham did give him the money in the presence of the people of Heth. Abraham showed that money was not as important an integrity and we should not be indebted to anyone except God. Abraham buried his wife Sarah in the cave of Machpelah near Mamre (Hebron) in the land of Canaan.

Genesis 24

Abraham was getting along in years and was concerned that a suitable wife be found for Isaac. He did not want his son to be drawn into pagan beliefs by marrying a daughter of the

Canaanites. He commissioned his eldest servant to return to
his country and to take a wife for Isaac from his kindred. The
servant had to place his hand under Abraham's thigh to seal
the bargain. This custom was a type of contract made prior
to the handshake. Today we have signed contracts on paper.
Ultimately it is a man's character and belief in absolute truth
which matters. If a man is not committed to God's moral
absolute of honesty, no contract, whether written, verbal, or
promised on a man's thigh is worth anything.

   The servant was concerned about his task, but Abraham
told him that the Lord would be with him and direct him to
the proper woman. The servant departed in a caravan of ten
camels and went to Mesopotamia to the city of Nahor where a
small remnant of Abraham's kinfolks still served the true God.
Abraham told his servant that if God did not provide Isaac's
mate he would be freed from the oath. The servant arrived with
his camels at the city well, at the time in the evening when the

Rebecca at the Source

Antonio Bellucci

women come to draw water for their households. The servant prayed to the Lord that Isaac's future wife would give him a drink and then offer to water all of his camels. This was an extremely unlikely event.

Before the servant had even finished praying, Rebekah, an unmarried virgin, came with her water pitcher upon her shoulder. She filled her pitcher and gave a drink to the stunned servant of Abraham. She proceeded to water all of his camels. Then the servant placed earrings and bracelets upon Rebekah and gave thanks to the Lord. Rebekah was born to Bethuel, the son of Milcah, the wife of Nahor, Abraham's brother. Rebekah was Isaac's first cousin. Again we see that in this early period of earth history, it was possible for close relations to be married with no apparent genetic problems. According to the bible Rebekah was very fair. I suspect this is Bible language for stunning, a real babe. God's provision always exceeds our every hope or dream.

The servant later explained all these things to Rebekah's family, who agreed that this was from the Lord. So they said, *"Behold, Rebekah is with you, take her and go, and let her be your master's son's wife, as the Lord has spoken."* When the servant heard these words he bowed himself to the ground and worshipped the Lord again. He then brought forth jewels of gold and clothing, giving them to Rebekah. He also gave Laban and Rebecca's mother many precious things. They wanted her to stay at home for awhile, but the servant requested that he return to his master immediately. This was undoubtedly wise. Once a clear course of action is revealed by God, any delay in obeying invariably causes problems.

Rebekah's family was understandably reluctant to send their daughter to a distant land on short notice but asked Rebekah what she wanted to do. Rebekah said she would go with the servant. So Abraham's servant brought Rebekah to be Isaac's bride. Isaac was meditating in the field at evening by the well Lahairol in the south. He lifted up his head and saw the camel caravan approaching. Rebekah saw Isaac and she dismounted from the camel and asked the servant, *"Who is this man that walked in the field to meet us?"*

The servant said, *"It is my master."* Hearing this, Rebekah took a veil and covered herself. The servant told Isaac all the things he had done. Isaac brought her into his mother Sarah's tent and Rebekah became his wife. Isaac loved Rebecca and was comforted by her after his mother's death. Who says marriages are not made in heaven?

Genesis 25

After Isaac's marriage to Rebekah, Abraham married Keturah (who like Hagar was considered a concubine). Keturah bore Abraham six sons in the 35 years Abraham was married to her. The only son that is well known from this union is Midan (whose descendants became the Midianites). The other sons probably mixed with descendants of Ishmael, Lot, and later with Esau's descendants to become the modern Arabic peoples. Abraham sent these sons eastward with adequate gifts so they could begin their own tribes. Abraham died at the age of 175 years. His father Terah died at the age of 205 years. This would indicate that human longevity has greatly declined since the flood.

Esau Sells his Birthright to Jacob

Abraham was buried with Sarah by his sons Isaac and Ishmael in the cave of Machpelah in the field of Ephron. Apparently Isaac and Ishmael had reconciled their differences in order to bury Abraham.

Verse 8 of Chapter 25 states that Abraham was gathered to his people. Since none of Abraham's ancestors were buried there, they must have been alive somewhere else. This is one of many scriptural clues that there

Rembrandt Harmensz. van Rijn - ca. 1648

is a life after our death. The question is whether we will live in the Lord's presence or eternally separated from our Lord (i.e.

hell). This place of departed spirits was later called "Abraham's Bosom" (See Luke 16:22). It came to pass that after the death of Abraham, God blessed Isaac and he lived by the well Lahairol.

Isaac was 40 years of age when he married Rebekah. Isaac petitioned the Lord for children because Rebekah appeared to be barren. The Lord answered his petition and she conceived twins. When the two babies struggled inside of her, she asked the Lord, *"Why is this so?"*

The Lord answered, *"You have two nations inside of your womb. The youngest of your sons will be the spiritual leader, and the elder shall serve the younger."* The first twin to be born was named Esau and he was covered with red hair like a garment. Jacob came out second and appeared to be grabbing Esau's heel during delivery. The name Esau means hairy and Jacob's name means heel-catcher (or supplanter). Esau became the hunter (like Nimrod) and Isaac showed Esau more favor because he enjoyed eating Esau's venison stew. Meanwhile, Rebecca favored Jacob who spent more time at home. This set the stage for sibling rivalry and family problems.

Esau came home from hunting very tired. He asked Jacob to fix him "red pottage", a boiled stew or soup. Jacob bargained with Esau for his birthright. Esau felt like he was dying so he said, *"What profit shall this birthright bring to me?"* So Esau sold his birthright to Jacob for bread and a pottage of lentils. Esau flippantly displayed a disregard for his birthright and family heritage.

Genesis 26

Due to famine, Isaac moved to the land of Gerar where Abimelech was still king of the Philistines. The Lord told Isaac to dwell there in the land of Egypt while the Lord multiplied his seed like the stars in heaven and again promised that all the nations of the earth would be blessed through his offspring. It may have been fifty years since the Lord had appeared to Isaac (when the Lord had previously confirmed his covenant made with Abraham and Isaac on Mount Moriah). The Lord had to provide Isaac special assurance for him and his family to go to Gerar in Egypt. The men in Gerar questioned Isaac about

Rebebkah because she was so beautiful. Fearing for his life and carrying on the family tradition, Isaac lied, "She is my sister."

When he saw Isaac fondling Rebekah, Abimelech asked, *"Surely Rebekah must be your wife?"* Isaac admitted that Rebekah was his wife. Abimelech was upset because if a Philistine male had lain with Rebekah he would have been guilty of adultery. It is obvious that even before Moses brought down the written Ten Commandments on tablets of clay that mankind already had God's moral laws written upon their hearts. So Abimelech decreed to his people that anyone who even touched Rebekah would be put to death.

Isaac farmed in Gerar and the Lord blessed him a hundred-fold. As a result, the Philistines envied Isaac and his possessions. They filled all the wells Abraham had previously dug. Even when Isaac moved away and dug new wells, the herdsmen of Gerar quarreled over the wells twice. Finally, Isaac dug a well he named Rehoboth because the Lord has made room for him and prospered him in this land. Isaac traveled to Beersheba. The Lord appeared to him there and said, *"I am the God of Abraham, your father, I am with thee, and I will bless thee and multiply your seed for my servant Abraham's sake."*

Isaac built an altar for the Lord, pitched his tent, and had his servants dig a new well. Abimelech came with his friend Ahuzzath and his captain Pichol. Isaac questioned, *"Why do you come to see me when you have sent me away from you?"*

They said, "We have certainly seen that the Lord is with you. Let us make an oath with you that you will do no harm to us because we have done nothing bad to you, but only sent you away in peace. We know now that you are blessed by the Lord. Isaac made them a feast and they ate and drank. Abimelech and his men rose in the morning, swore to Isaac that they would remain friends, and departed in peace. That same day Isaac's servants told him about another new well. Isaac named this well Shibah and to this day, the city is called Beershebah.

At this time, Esau was 40 years old and had married both Judith, the daughter of Beerl, the Hittite and Bashemath, the daughter of Elon, another Hittite. This grieved Isaac and Rebekah who wanted Esau to marry someone of his faith.

Marrying someone who does not share your belief about God is a recipe for disaster.

Genesis 27

As Isaac grew old, he eventually went blind. He called his favorite son Esau to him and said, *"My son, I am now old and near death. Take your bow and arrows and go into the field and get me some venison. Make me some savory meat which I love, bring it to me that I may eat, and then I will bless you before I die."* Rebecca overheard this and commanded Jacob to fetch two young goats from which she made Isaac some savory stew. She told Jacob to bring his father the meal before Esau returned so that Isaac would bless Jacob instead of Esau.

Instead of objecting to the deception, Jacob stated, *"My father will recognize me because I am not hairy like my brother. When he recognizes who I am, he will curse me rather than give me his blessing."* Jacob should have objected on principle instead of making

Isaac Blesses Jacob

Govert Flinck - 1638

excuses. Excuses can always be eliminated; principles cannot.

Rebekah said, *"Upon me will be the curse, so obey my voice and do as you are told."* Rebecca placed goat skins upon his arms and neck so that he would feel hairy like Esau. With the stew, Jacob entered his blind father's tent.

Isaac asked, *"Who are you, my son?"*

Jacob lied, *"I am Esau, your first born. I have done as you requested. Eat my venison so that you may bless me."*

Then Isaac said to his son, *"How is it that you found the meat so quickly, my son?"*

Jacob lied again, *"Because the Lord our God brought it to me."*

Isaac said, *"Come near me so that I may feel you and know you are my son Esau."*

After touching Jacob, Isaac said, *"The voice is like Jacob's but the hands are the hands of Esau."*

Isaac again questioned, *"Are you really my son Esau?"*

For the third time, Jacob lied, *"I am."*

Isaac ate the venison and blessed Jacob instead of Esau. Isaac said, *"Let all people serve you and all nations bow down to you. You will be lord over your brothers and they will bow down to you. And blessed be those who bless you"*

As soon as Isaac had finished with the blessing, Esau returned from hunting. He also made a savory stew for his father Isaac. Then Esau entered Isaac's tent. Isaac asked, *"Who are you?"*

Esau answered, *"I am your first born son Esau."*

Trembling, Isaac said, *"Who was it that just brought the venison to me? I have eaten before you came and blessed him. The blessing will remain."*

Esau was very upset and requested that his father bless him too. Isaac said, *"Your brother came with lies and deceit and has taken away your blessing."*

Esau said, *"Jacob has taken two things from me: my birthright and now my blessing. Have you not reserved a blessing for me?"*

Isaac answered, *"I have made him Lord over you. I have blessed him with grain and wine. What can I do for you, my son?"*

Esau said, *"Have you only one blessing; if not, bless me also."* Esau lifted up his voice and cried.

Isaac said, *"Your dwelling will be away from the earth's richness. You will live by the sword and you will serve your brother."*

Holding a grudge, Esau said, *"The days of mourning for my father are at hand. When they are over, I will kill my brother Jacob."*

Rebekah overheard Esau's plot and told Jacob to run away and live with her brother in Haran. Rebekah said, *"When your brother's anger is over, I'll send word for you to come back."*

Lies, deceit, and favoritism had torn the family apart.

Genesis 28

Rebekah said to Isaac, *"I am weary of my life because of the daughters of Heth. If Jacob takes a wife of the daughters of Heth, such as these which are in the land, what good will my life be to me?"*

Isaac blessed Jacob and said, *"You will not take a wife of the daughters of Canaan. Go to Padanaram, to the house of Bethuel, your mother's father, and take a wife from one of the daughters of Laban, your mother's brother."* Jacob did as his father instructed. Esau realized that his parents were not pleased that he had married two daughters of the Canaanites.

Jacob left Beersheba and traveled to Haran. Night came and he used a stone for a pillow as he lay down to sleep. He dreamed of a ladder reaching up to heaven with angels from God ascending and descending on it. Above the ladder, Jacob saw the Lord who said, *"I am the Lord, God of your father Abraham and the God of Isaac and upon the land which you are lying upon, and I will give it to you and all of your off-spring. They will spread all over the Earth, and be blessed through you. I will be with you wherever you go, and will not leave you until all has been done of which I have spoken to you."*

Jacob awoke and said, *"Surely the Lord is here and I knew it not. This place is none other than the house of God and is the gate of Heaven,"* and he was afraid. He used the stone from his pillow and built a pillar and poured oil upon it. Although the place was originally called Luz, Jacob renamed it Bethel. Jacob said, *"If God will be with me and give me bread and clothing so that I can go to my father's house in peace, then the Lord shall be my God. This stone I have set up as a pillar shall be God's house and all that the Lord will bless me with, I will give a tenth back."* (This is the second time the tithe is mentioned in the

Jacob's Dream

Ferdinand Bol - 1642

33

Bible. The first place is Genesis 14:20 where Abraham gave
tithes to Melchizedek.)

Genesis 29

Jacob came upon Haran and saw a well in the field where
the animals were watered. A large stone was placed over the
well's mouth so that the animals would not fall in. Jacob met
people at the well and asked them if they knew Laban of Haran.
They did and they told him that even now Laban's daughter
Rachel was coming with sheep. Jacob rolled away the stone so
Rachel could water the sheep. Glad to have found relatives,
Jacob kissed Rachel, lifted up his voice to praise God, and wept.
Jacob told Rachel that he was her father's relative and Rebekah's
son. Rachel ran to her father and told him these things. Laban
ran to meet Jacob, embraced him, kissed him, and brought him
to his home. Jacob told Laban all about himself and his family.
Laban invited Jacob to work for him and asked what wages
Jacob would request.

Now Laban had two daughters, the oldest being Leah and
the youngest Rachel. Leah had tender eyes (probably meaning
poor eyesight), but Rachel was beautiful. Jacob had already
fallen in love with Rachel so he said, *"I will work for you for seven
years so that I may marry Rachel."*

Laban said, *"It is better for you to have her than another man, so stay
and work for me."* When the seven years were completed, Jacob
said it was time to marry Rachel. Laban gathered his entire
household and prepared a great wedding feast. Late at night
after the feast, Laban brought Leah into Jacob's room rather
than Rachel. Jacob's deceit with his own father had come full
circle. As a result of Laban's deceit, Jacob consummated his
marriage by having sex with the wrong woman. We really do
reap what we sow.

In the morning, Jacob awoke and realized he had slept with
Leah instead of Rachel. He was a very unhappy camper. He
went to Laban and said, *"What is this you have done to me? Did I not
serve you seven years for Rachel?"*

Laban answered, *"In our country, the rule is that the oldest daughter
must first be given in marriage before the younger. Agree to work another
seven years for Rachel and you can have her in one week."* Rachel was

given to Jacob who worked another seven years for Laban. In all likelihood, Laban's real goal was to keep Jacob as his employee because Jacob had brought him great prosperity. Because Jacob loved Rachel more than Leah, the Lord had mercy upon Leah and gave her four sons: Reuben, Simeon, Levi, and Judah. Rachel seemed unable to have children. In the culture of that day, a woman with sons was greatly valued whereas a barren woman was considered worthless. It was through the line of the fourth son of Leah and Jacob, Judah, that the savior of humanity would ultimately come to earth. One of Christ's many titles is the "Lion from the Tribe of Judah".

Genesis 30

Rachel was upset because she bore no children, blaming it upon Jacob. Angrily Jacob said, *"Am I God who has withheld the fruit of your womb?"* Rachel then told Jacob to sleep with Bilhah, her maid, so that she could give Jacob children (history seems to repeat itself). Having children through servants and calling them your own was a common custom in the world at that time. Through Bilhah, Jacob bore Rachel's sons whom she named Dan and Naphtali. Leah bore no more children so she became upset when she saw that Rachel was being given sons through her maid. So she requested Jacob to sleep with her maid Zilpah. Zilpah bore two more sons Gad and Asher to Jacob.

Ruben, Leah's oldest son, found some mandrakes in the field during the wheat harvest and brought them to his mother. Rachel requested the mandrakes from Leah. Leah said, *"You have taken away my husband, now you also want my son's mandrakes?"*

Rachel said, *"For the mandrakes, you can lay with Jacob tonight."*

Leah ran out to meet Jacob and said, *"You must come with me because I have hired you to sleep with me."* Jacob did and Leah conceived and bore a son she named Issachar. Later Leah conceived again and bore Jacob a sixth son named Zebulun. She also conceived and bore a daughter she named Dinah.

In God's timing, Rachel's womb was opened and she bore Jacob a son named Joseph. Since Rachael had always remained Jacob's true love, it was obvious to everyone that Joseph was his favorite child. This favoritism would later have disastrous results. One lesson here is that God loves all of us with equal passion. The fact that we are treated differently has nothing to do with his love for us but rather our needing different treatment because we are different people. On the other hand, Jacob publicly treated Joseph differently because he loved him more than his other sons.

Eventually Jacob requested to return to his own homeland. Because Jacob was very prosperous however, Laban asked him to stay. Jacob responded, *"I need to provide for my household as well."*

Laban said, *"What can I give you to stay?"* Jacob proposed a plan where he would feed and care for the entire flock. His payment would be all of the speckled, spotted, or dark sheep and goats. All those animals without blemishes would be Laban's. Laban answered and said, *"Behold I agree according to thy word."* Jacob made the separation of the animals according to his word and placed all of his flock three days journey away from Laban's flock. Being an experienced shepherd and stock breeder, Jacob knew that Laban's flock contained heterozygous genes even though all appeared to be homozygous. Jacob prepared a way to have the strong animals conceive at the watering troughs. Many speckled or spotted lambs were born. When the feeble animals came to drink, Jacob would remove the rods from the watering troughs so none of the weaker animals conceived. Jacob had a strong healthy herd while Laban ended up with the weaker animals. Thus, Jacob increased in wealth with large flocks and many servants.

Genesis 31

Because of Jacob's increasing prosperity, Laban's sons said that Jacob had stolen all of their father's wealth. Jacob heard the Lord tell him to return to the land of his father. So Jacob called Rachel and Leah and told them that although he had served their father well, Laban's behavior had changed toward him. Jacob said, *"Your father has deceived me and has changed my wages ten times. Yet the Lord has been with me and has protected me from him. As you can see, God has taken away the livestock of your father and given them to me."*

The Lord stated to Jacob, *"I am the God of Bethel where you vowed a vow to me; now get out of this land and return to the land of your father."* Rachel and Leah were understandably upset about leaving their home. They asked many questions such as, *"Isn't there any portion or inheritance left in our father's house for us? Are we not now counted as strangers? He has sold us and devoured that money as well."* They agreed to Jacob's plan and said, *"Surely all the riches God has taken from our father belong to us and our children. Do whatever God has told you to do."* So Jacob rose up, set his wives and sons upon the camels, gathered all his animals acquired in Padanaram, and headed back to Canaan, his father Isaac's land.

Jacob left with his wives, children, and possessions. Approximately three days later, Laban was shearing sheep when he was told that Jacob had fled with his carved idols. Laban immediately pursued Jacob and caught up to him at Mount Gilead. The Lord came to Laban in a dream and advised him to do neither good nor bad to Jacob. Laban confronted Jacob and asked him why he had stolen away with his daughters, saying he would have liked to send them off with a party. He then accused Jacob of stealing his property. Jacob swore to kill whoever had stolen Laban's gods. Jacob did not know that it was Rachel.

Laban searched all of Jacob's tents but did not find them because Rachel was sitting on the gods in the camel's seat. Asking her father's forgiveness, Rachel said it was her menstrual time and did not come down from the camel. Then Jacob confronted Laban and said, *"What have I done and what is my sin that you have so hotly pursued after me? You have searched all of my belongings and have found nothing of yours. Twenty years I have toiled for you. I served fourteen years for your daughters, six years for your cattle and in the process you changed my wages ten times."*

Laban answered, *"These daughters are my daughters, these children are my children, these cattle are my cattle, and all you can see is mine. What can I do this day to my daughters and to the children they have born. So let us make a covenant between the two of us."* Jacob took a stone and set it up for a pillar. Jacob also asked his relatives to gather stones into a heap. Then they all ate upon the heap of stones which Laban named Jegar Sahadutha. However, Jacob called it Galeed.

It was also called Mizpah because Laban said, *"The Lord will watch over us when we are absent from one another. You will not afflict my daughters or take any other wives besides them. Even though no man is*

*with us, God is a witness between you and me. Let this heap and pillar be
a witness that you will not pass over them to cause me harm. May the God
of Abraham, the God of Nahor, and the God of their father judge between
us.*" Jacob swore to this oath by the fear of his father Isaac.
Then Jacob offered a sacrifice and they all ate a meal and spent
the night. Laban arose early in the morning, kissed his grandchildren and daughters, and blessed them before he returned to
Haran.

Genesis 32

Because his twin brother had sworn to kill him, Jacob was
extremely terrified of the coming encounter with Esau. Jacob
sent ahead messengers to meet with his brother Esau, in the
land of Seir, which is the country of Edom. He commanded
the messengers to speak in reverence to Esau. Jacob requested
mercy from Esau and also told the messengers to state that he
was returning to the land of our Father.

The messengers returned to Jacob reporting that they had
met with Esau who was coming with four hundred armed men.
Jacob was petrified. He divided his people and animals into two
groups. His plan was to send the first group ahead to meet Esau
and his men. If Esau destroyed them, the second group would
escape. Then Jacob prayed to the Lord. Probably for the first
time in his life, Jacob relied totally on the mercy of God rather
than his own conniving. He acknowledged to God he was not
worthy of His mercies. In his prayer, Jacob acknowledged that
all of God's blessings he received were only by God's grace. He
asked that the Lord protect him from his brother Esau. to spare
his people because he had been obedient when God had told
him to return. Jacob even reminded the Lord of His promise
that Jacob's seed would be like the sand of the sea, which cannot
be counted. He asked God to fulfill his word even though the
outward circumstances appeared hopeless. No prayer could be
truly effective unless it agreed with God's revealed word.

Jacob prepared a present for his servants to give to Esau.
The present was twenty male goats, two hundred female goats,
two hundred ewes, twenty rams, thirty female camels with
their young, forty cows, ten bulls, twenty female donkeys and
ten male donkeys. He commanded his servants to gather each

herd of animals by itself keeping space between them. He also commanded them to tell Esau that each herd was a gift from Jacob. The servants left with the flocks. Jacob rose up that night, took his two wives, their maidservants with his eleven sons and daughter, and sent them over the river at Jabbok.

Alone, Jacob wrestled with "a man" until the break of day. When the wrestler saw that he could not prevail over Jacob, he touched Jacobs's thigh and forced it out of joint. (This man was actually an angel, the pre-incarnate Christ). Jacob recognized that he had seen God face to face. As he had held on to Esau's heel at birth, he now held on to God, so earnest was his desire for God's purpose to be accomplished in and through him. During this encounter God asked Jacob, *"What is your name?"*

He answered, *"Jacob."*

Jacob Wrestling with the Angel

Rembrandt Harmensz. van Rijn - ca. 1659

God said, *"Your name shall no longer be called Jacob but Israel for you have struggled with God and men and have overcome."* God then blessed Jacob. Once Jacob finally learned to rely completely upon God, he became a new creation with a new name (like we all can).

Jacob named the place Peniel because he had seen God face to face and his life was preserved. (The name Israel can mean either *"one who fights victoriously with God"* or *"a prevailing prince with God"*). Leaving Peniel, Jacob limped for the rest of his life because of his hip, a reminder of his dependence upon God. Commemorating Jacob's experience with God, the Israelites to this day do not eat the tendon attached to the hip socket.

Genesis 33

Jacob saw Esau coming with his four hundred men. He divided the children unto Leah and Rachel and the two handmaidens. Jacob placed the handmaidens and their children first, Leah and her children next, and Rachel and Joseph in the rear. Quickly falling back into his old ways, he organized them by the value he placed upon them. Traveling on ahead, Jacob bowed down seven times as he approached his brother. Esau ran to meet him, embraced him, and kissed him. They wept. Esau saw the women and children and asked, *"Who are these that are with you?"*

Jacob said, *"They are the children which God has so graciously given to me."* The handmaidens and their children came and bowed before Esau, as did Leah and her children. Jacob went near Rachel and Joseph and they bowed down also.

Esau asked, *"What is meant by these droves of animals?"*

Jacob answered, *"They are intended for you, my lord."*

Esau said, *"I have enough of my own, my brother; you keep them for yourself."* Realizing that God had blessed him abundantly and that his resources were inexhaustible, Jacob insisted that Esau receive his gift as a token of his love. So Esau kept the animals.

Since Jacob was concerned for the young children and animals, he decided to travel at a slower pace than Esau. Esau said, *"Then let me leave you some of my men."* Jacob declined and journeyed to Succoth. He built a house there and booths for his cattle. Then Jacob went to Shalem where he pitched his tent before the city. Jacob purchased land for a hundred pieces of silver from the sons of Hamar and then he erected an altar for the Lord and named it Eleloheisrael. As with most worries, his concern that Esau would kill him was unfounded. He wisely depended upon God and the Lord had brought him through his troubles.

Genesis 34

Dinah, Jacob's daughter by Leah, was out walking in the countryside. Shechem, one of the sons of Hamor, saw her beauty and raped her. Afterward, Shechem wanted Dinah as his wife and asked his father Hamor to get her. When Jacob's sons learned that Dinah had been defiled and that Shechem wanted to marry her, they were filled with grief and fury. So Dinah's brothers decided to take things into their own hands. They told Shechem that they could not give their sister to an uncircumcised man. But if all the men of the city would agree to be circumcised, Dinah's brothers would consent to give her away and they would intermarry. Hamor and Shechem agreed because Shechem took great delight in Dinah and Jacob's family who were obviously very rich. The two went into their city and convinced all the males to be circumcised by telling them everything Jacob owned would become theirs. All were circumcised and three days later when the men were in great pain, Simeon and Levi took Dinah out of Shechem's house and murdered every man in the city. Then they plundered the city taking all the possessions, animals, women, and children.

Jacob was troubled over what Simeon and Levi had done. Jacob stated that Simeon and Levi gave him a very bad reputation among the Canaanites and Perizzites. Jacob said, *"We are few in number; they will gather together and destroy us."*

His sons' said, *"Should we have let them deal with our sister as though she were a harlot?"* Jacob knew what they had done was not God's will but did nothing to discipline his sons.

Genesis 35

God told Jacob to settle in Bethel and build an altar there to God. Jacob had all his household put away their strange gods, purify themselves, and change their garments. They gave Jacob all their foreign gods and their earrings and Jacob buried them underneath an oak near Shechem. God protected them from the cities and people around them, and they were not pursued. They came to Luz in the land of Canaan. Jacob built an altar and named it Elbethel because God had appeared to him there when he was fleeing from his brother Esau. God appeared again to Jacob and blessed him. Then God told Jacob that his name would be Israel. He also told Jacob to be fruitful and multiply because nations and kings would come from him. Furthermore, the land God gave to Abraham and Isaac was now given to Jacob and his descendants. Jacob named this place Bethel.

On the way to Bethlehem, Rachel started a very difficult labor. The midwife told her not to fear because she would give birth to a second son. Rachel died in childbirth and as her spirit and soul departed she named her son Benoni. Jacob renamed this son Benjamin and Rachel was buried in Bethlehem. Rachel died where Jesus was to be born as prophesied in Micah 5:2. Rachel's son Benjamin (meaning *"son of my right hand,"* first named Benoni meaning *"son of pain"*) was the progenitor of the tribe that would eventually inhabit this portion of the Promised Land. The phrase, *"Rachel weeping for her children"* (see Jeremiah 31:15 and Matthew 2:18) refers to Herod slaying all the male children of Bethlehem.

Israel (the former Jacob) journeyed and spread his tent beyond the tower of Edar. Israel learned that his oldest son Reuben had slept with Bilhah, his father's concubine. All of Israel's twelve sons and their birth mothers are listed. The death of Isaac is also recorded with Jacob and Esau burying their father (which was previously covered).

Genesis 36

This chapter covers the generations of Esau, the father of the Edomites of Mount Seir. This toledoth (toledoth is the Hebrew word meaning the story or generational history of a family) of Esau was probably acquired by Israel (formerly Jacob) at their father's burial. It appears that Israel appended it to his own toledoth just before affixing his closing signature in Genesis 37:2.

Esau married forty years before Israel; more than one generation of descendents is recorded. Also recorded are the sons of Seir, a Horite who had originally settled in the Mount Seir region. This region was later known as Edom, another name for Esau meaning red. Esau's descendents had partially conquered the Horites by this time. The remainder of this chapter appears to have been inserted by Moses at the time of the Exodus, since he knew that the Israelites would be encountering the Edomites when they left the wilderness. Moses also knew that the Israelites would eventually have a king (Deuteronomy 17:14-20) even though they did not have one in his day

part 5

Genesis 37 to 50
Joseph —A precursor for Christ

Genesis 37

The Genesis narrative now slows down and concentrates on the life of one man – Jacob's favorite son, Joseph. The historical account begins with the jealously of Joseph's brothers. Joseph, a seventeen year old, was in charge of tending the flocks with his brothers. Since Joseph had been born to Rachael, Jacob's true love, in his old age, Jacob loved Joseph more than his other children. He made Joseph a coat of many colors. By this action (and probably for many other reasons), it was obvious that Joseph was their father's favorite. Joseph's brothers hated him and did not speak nicely to him.

Joseph had a dream which made them hate him even more. He told his brothers that in his dream they were all binding sheaves in the field when Joseph's sheaf arose and stood upright. All their sheaves gathered around and bowed down to Joseph's sheaf. His brothers said, *"Will you reign over us?"*

Joseph had a second dream in which the sun, moon and eleven stars were in obedience to him. Upon telling these dreams to his brothers and his father, Israel said, *"Will your mother and I along with your brothers come to bow down to you?"* His brothers were jealous and hated him even more but his father kept his dream under observation. Joseph's two dreams were apparently from God because they were indeed ultimately fulfilled. However, his method of revealing them to his family lacked humility and discretion.

His brothers returned to tend the flock. Israel sent Joseph to join his brothers but also requested that Joseph report back on his brothers and the flock, in essence acting as a spy. Joseph went looking for his brothers and finally found them in Dothan. His brothers saw him coming, conspired to kill him, and said, *"Here comes the dreamer. Let us slay him and throw him into a pit and say that an evil beast has devoured him and then we will see what becomes of his dreams."*

Joseph is Pulled Out of the Well

Anonymous

Ruben heard of this plan and said, *"Let us not kill him; we do not want to shed any blood. We will just throw him into a pit in the wilderness."* Ruben planned to return later and let Joseph out.

After Ruben left, the others stripped Joseph of his colored coat and cast him into a pit. The brothers sat down to eat when a caravan of Ishmaelites came along with spices, balm, and myrrh to sell in Egypt. Judah said, *"What profit is it for us to slay our brother and conceal his blood? Let us sell him to the Ishmaelites, so we are not harming our own flesh and blood."* His brothers consented and sold Joseph for twenty pieces of silver. The Ishmaelites took Joseph into Egypt.

Rueben returned to the pit and did not find Joseph. His brothers killed a goat, sprinkled its blood on the colored coat, and brought it to their father. They said, *"We have found this coat but not Joseph. He must have been devoured by a wild animal."* When Israel saw Joseph's bloodied coat, he put on sackcloth and mourned for Joseph for many days. Everyone tried but no one could comfort Israel.

He said, *"I will go into my grave still mourning my son Joseph."* Meanwhile, Joseph was sold in Egypt to Potiphar, the captain of Pharaoh's guards. Potiphar, like Pharaoh, was a title in Egypt rather than a personal name.

Genesis 38

Chapter 38 takes a detour from Joseph's history to reveal the character of several people involved in the direct line from Abraham to Jesus Christ. Judah left his brothers and married Shuah, a Canaanite woman, who bore him three sons named

Judah and Tamar

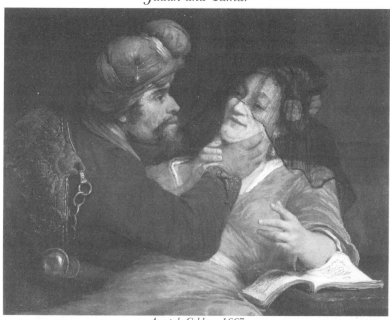

Arent de Gelder - 1667

Er, Oman and Shelah. Judah selected Tamar to be the wife of his oldest son Er. In this chapter, it is revealed that Tamar had a son by Judah, her father-in-law, through a rather involved and unsavory intrigue. Yet Tamar was the first of four women (the others were Rahab, Ruth, and Bathsheba) listed directly in the genealogy of Jesus Christ.

When Er died, it was Jewish law that the second son Oman would become her husband. He did not like this plan and treated Tamar badly. God put Oman to death. Judah's only remaining son Shelah was next in line to marry Tamar. Judah slighted her and did not allow the marriage. To get back at Judah for breaking Jewish law, Tamar disguised herself as a prostitute and slept with her father-in-law for the price of his staff, signet ring, and bracelet. She became pregnant. When Judah learned that Tamar was pregnant, he planned to have her burned to death for adultery. Tamar confronted Judah with his own staff, signet ring, and bracelet. Judah realized he was the father and acknowledged that Tamar had been more righteous than he.

Tamar gave birth to twin sons and Perez, one of the sons, was in the royal line leading to Jesus. God chose to come to earth representing all of humanity - not just the lily white, pure, and holy. His family line consists of murderers and prostitutes...liars and thieves...Jews and non-Jews...royalty and paupers...men and women...the righteous and sinners. Jesus came to save all of humanity and his lineage includes all of humanity.

Genesis 39

Back to the narrative of Joseph, he was still trapped in Egypt but had became a prosperous and influential man working for a wealthy man named Potiphar. Potiphar saw that God had blessed Joseph and trusted him implicitly. The Pharaoh's men who accepted high positions were required to become Eunuchs. This may have caused the adulterous desires of Potiphar's wife or it may have simply been her sinful nature. Either way she burned with desire for Joseph who was apparently a good looking young man. In the mean time, Joseph had become a godly person and well favored in Potiphar's household. Potiphar's wife knew that Joseph was not a Eunuch and pressed hard to have an affair with him. But Joseph was a righteous man who cared more about honoring God than the desires of the flesh. Therefore he repeatedly refused the advances from another man's wife.

Joseph Accused by Potiphar's Wife

Rembrandt Harmensz. van Rijn - 1655

Eventually Potiphar's wife became humiliated by Joseph's refusal to have sex with her and her desire turned to vindictiveness. She accused him of sexually attacking her - resulting in him being sent to Pharaoh's prison. The penalty for such an act should have been death, leading many to speculate that Potiphar may not have been totally convinced by his wife's lies but still needed to "save face". In spite of yet another setback Joseph did not despair but again accepted his fate and worked hard in the situation in which he now found himself. The Lord gave Joseph favor in the sight of the keeper of the prison leaders, and eventually Joseph was placed in charge of all the other prisoners. Joseph's integrity allowed the warden to let Joseph run the prison without any concern that he would abuse or misuse the confidence placed upon him.

Genesis 40

In this chapter we learn that Joseph continues to be able to interpret dreams – both his own and those of others which come from the Lord. A baker and a butler are both thrown into prison, apparently for a plot to kill the pharaoh. Both have strange dreams which reveal the immediate future for their lives. Joseph interprets in exact detail what both dreams mean and both dreams come true just as Joseph predicted - resulting in the release and vindication of the butler (or cupbearer) and the death of the baker. The butler had promised to remember Joseph upon his release from prison but promptly forgot him once released. Joseph again reveals the depth of his character by continuing in jail for two more years with no indication of bitterness. Joseph never lost hope even though those around him continue to break their promises and he was being persecuted without any apparent reason.

Genesis 41

This chapter covers Joseph's release from prison to interpret Pharaoh's dream. Pharaoh has a very disturbing dream which no-one can interpret. The butler finally remembers Joseph as a "dream interpreter" and tells the Pharaoh of his experience in jail. So the Pharaoh has Joseph released from prison to interpret his dream. Significantly, Joseph immediately says it is not him who knows the meaning of the dream but God who reveals those truths to him – giving the Lord all the credit rather than claiming any glory for himself. Joseph tells Pharaoh that the dream reveals that there will be seven years of bountiful crops followed by seven years of famine. Joseph was not embarrassed or hesitant to speak again and again about the true God of creation who controls all things. Joseph goes on to tell the Pharaoh exactly what needs to be done to prevent a national disaster. As a result Pharaoh acknowledged God and recognizes that the spirit of God was with Joseph. Joseph became Pharaoh's "right-hand" man.

Egyptian chronology and the identity of the various Pharaohs mentioned in the Bible are unsettled but there are several periods of Egyptian decline which may correspond to this period in world history. Historical records of the ancient historians and the archaeological inscriptions outside of God's Word are highly self-serving and are of uncertain reliability. Our biblical records come from men God inspired to record all of God's truth. These events happened almost 4000 years ago so it is not at all surprising that there is some conflict between the exact chronology recorded by the Bible (which has been meticulously maintained, copied, and guarded) and other historical interpretations. For the most part, every historical verse of the Bible has been confirmed by archaeological and other historical confirmations. Cities and people mentioned in Genesis which for decades were not even believed to have existed have almost ultimately been found to be absolute facts.

Pharaoh set Joseph over all the land of Egypt. He gave Joseph his signet ring, vestures of fine linen, and placed a gold chain around his neck. He made Joseph ride in the second chariot, and all bowed down before Joseph just as if he had

Joseph Distributing Corn in Egypt

Bartholomeus Breenbergh - 1655

the same authority as Pharaoh. Pharaoh told Joseph, *"I am Pharaoh and without thee shall no man lift up his hand or foot in all the land of Egypt."* The Pharaoh called Joseph Zaphnathpaaneah (perhaps meaning "God speaks, giving life to the World".) Pharaoh gave Joseph an Egyptian wife named Asenath, the daughter of Potipherah, priest of On. Joseph was thirty years old when he stood before Pharaoh, king of Egypt. He had spent over 12 years in bondage and prison with no realistic hope of release. Yet he never doubted that God was sovereign over his life and ultimately ended up as the second most powerful man upon the earth.

During the seven years of plenty Joseph developed a plan to store the excess grain in preparation for the years of famine. Thus when the famine came he was prepared and sold the grain back to the people – acquiring enormous wealth for the government of Egypt. All the surrounding countries sent representatives to buy corn and grain from Joseph because the famine was also affecting their lands.

Genesis 42

Because the famine was so widespread, Joseph's brothers came to Egypt to purchase grain. Benjamin, the youngest of all the brothers, was not allowed to come because Israel did not want to lose him - like he thought he had lost Joseph. When his brothers arrived they bowed down to Joseph without recognizing him. This was an exact fulfillment of his dream from many years earlier. Joseph acted hostile in order to test their character. He said, *"You are spies coming to see the nakedness of our land."* They responded, *"No my Lord, we only came to buy food."* *"We are all brothers from one father and our father is at home with our youngest brother and one of our brothers is no more."* Joseph still insisted that they were spies. He told them that to prove they were not, one brother must go back and get their youngest brother. Joseph placed them all in prison for three days. Joseph wanted to find out if his brothers resented Benjamin, like they had resented him because their mother was Rachel. Joseph listened while they confessed their sin, and this is what he wanted to hear. They assumed Joseph would not know Hebrew because of the very different languages which had been formed across the earth ever since people dispersed from the Tower of Babel. However, Joseph understood everything his brothers were saying. Joseph had to leave his brothers to go and weep to relieve his emotions before continuing in conversation. Joseph longed to be reconciled to his family, but he had to be certain his brothers were sincere in their attitudes, so he subjected them to a number of tests. After hearing them express regret in their previous actions, Joseph took Simeon hostage and sent the other brothers with the grain back to their homes to fetch Benjamin.

Joseph bound Simeon before their eyes. He did this because it was Simeon who was instrumental in their actions against Joseph previously. Joseph had their sacks filled with grain and sent them on their way. On their way back they opened a sack of donkey feed and found the money given to buy the grain. They were afraid, saying one to another, *"What is this that God has done to us?"* Upon emptying their sacks all the brothers found their money, which they thought they had paid to purchase the grain. They told their father Israel everything which had happened including the need to leave Simeon and the request to return with Benjamin. Israel said, *"I am bereaved for my children, Joseph is gone, now Simeon, and you are against me."* Ruben said, *"If we did not bring Benjamin back then two sons will be lost, but, if you do I will return your son back to you."* Israel said, *"My son will not go with you, one son is already dead and something might happen to my son Benjamin, which shall bring down my grey hairs and sorrow into my grave should I lose him also."* So Israel refused to send them back.

Genesis 43

The famine continued in the land of Canaan. With their food gone, again Israel relented and told his sons to go again to buy them more food. Judah told Israel that the man in charge of all the food said, *"You shall not see me if you come back without Benjamin."* *"If Benjamin is not with us when we go we will not go."*

Israel said, *"Why did you have to tell this man about your youngest brother?"* They answered, *"This man specifically asked us about our family. How were we to know he would request us to bring our youngest brother with us when we returned?"* Judah said, *"Send Benjamin with me and my brothers so we will all not die for lack of food."* So Israel told them to take double the money along with a little honey, spices, myrrh, nuts and almonds as a gift for this man. *"May God almighty be with you before this man and if something happens that he does not release your other brother and keeps Benjamin, I will be bereaved of my children."*

The other sons of Jacob left with everything and again stood before Joseph. When Joseph saw his brothers with Benjamin he said to the ruler of his house, *"Bring these men to my home, slay and make ready a feast for these men for they shall dine with me at noon."* Joseph's servant did as he was told and brought the men into Joseph's house. They were afraid, remembering what had happened before, since the money had not been taken for the grain, he could take all of their possessions. So they told the servant what had happened in the past. The servant said, *"I placed the money back into your sack."* He brought their brother Simeon to them, brought them into Joseph's house, and gave them water to wash their feet. So the brothers prepared their gifts to give Joseph.

When Joseph arrived they presented him with their gifts and bowed themselves to him. Joseph asked if their father, the old man they spoke of, was still alive. They said he was and is in good health.

Joseph saw his brother Benjamin and asked, *"Is this the younger brother you spoke of,"* and added, *"God be gracious unto thee, my son."* Joseph left in haste and entered his chamber to weep because he could not contain his emotions. He washed his face came back to his brothers and said, *"Let us sit down to eat of bread."* They sat down with Joseph to eat and noticed that they had been seated according to their birth order, the youngest first with the others in that order. They marveled at this coincidence. (The odds of them being seated by age would have been 39,917,000 to one). Joseph gave them food with Benjamin's quantity being five times as much as the others as one last test to see if they were still filled with jealousy and would treat him with distain.

Genesis 44

After the meal the steward filled all the men's sacks with grain and placed each man's money into the top of their sacks again (as instructed by Joseph). The next morning they were all sent away and Joseph instructed his steward to take some men and overtake them and tell them, *"Why have you rewarded evil for good?" "Didn't my Lord eat and drink with you from a silver divining cup?"* This cup had been placed into Benjamin's sack. The servant said to the men, *"With whosoever this cup is found will die or become my Lord's bond servant, the rest of you will be blame-*

Judah and Joseph

Arent de Gelder - ca. 1680-1685

less." All the sacks were searched and the cup was found in Benjamin's sack. All the brother's tore their clothes in sorrow and turned their animals around, heading back to see Joseph.

Judah was the first to reach Joseph's house and fell to the ground before Joseph. Joseph asked, *"What have you done that have made you return to my audience?"* Judah said, *"What shall we say and how shall we speak to you Lord? God has found iniquity in us your servants, not only in us, but in the man's sack with whom the cup was found."* Judah came closer to Joseph and said, *"May I speak in my Lord's ear and let not your anger burn against us, for truly you are even like the Pharaoh. You asked us before if we had a father or any other brothers and we told you the truth. We said we had a father and younger brother in Canaan and that one of our brothers is dead. This younger brother is the only one left of his mother, and his father loves him dearly."* You asked us to bring him down with us and we did. His father didn't want to let him come with us but you my Lord said, *"Do not come back without him."* His father said, *"I will most certainly die if I do not see him again. My wife bore me two sons, the one was torn to pieces by a wild animal, and I have not seen him since, and if I lose the other one, it will bring down my gray hairs and sorrow into my grave."* Judah asked Joseph to let him be the bondservant and let Benjamin go back with his brothers to their father. I ask you Lord, *"How can I go back to my father if the lad Benjamin is not with me, Lest I see the evil that it will bring to my father?"*

Genesis 45

At this point Joseph could no longer contain himself so he sent away all of his servants and was alone with his brothers. He made himself known unto his brothers and wept aloud so hard that the entire house of the Pharaoh heard. He told his brothers, *"I am Joseph, does my father still live?"* His brothers could not answer him immediately because they were in shock. Joseph told them to come closer and not to be grieved or be afraid because God had sent him ahead to preserve their lives. *"We have had famine for two years and there will be another five years before this famine will end. God has made me a father to Pharaoh, Lord of his house and ruler throughout the land of Egypt. Go and tell our father this, and tell him and all of his family to come on down to Egypt and tarry not. You can live in the land of Goshen so you can be near me, your children, your children's children, your flocks, your herds, and every-thing that you own. I will nourish you all through the next five years of famine, so you will not end up in poverty. Tell our father of all the glory God has given me and tell him to make haste and come down to Egypt."*

Joseph and Benjamin hugged each other and wept. Joseph also hugged and wept with all of his brothers and they had a very long conversation. All in Pharaoh's house heard of the reunion and were happy for Joseph. The Pharaoh instructed Joseph to have his brothers take beasts and bring their families from Canaan saying, *"I will give them all the good of this land of Egypt and they shall live off of the fat of this land. Take wagons for the little ones and for their wives, and bring your father and come."* So the children of Israel did as they were instructed and returned to Egypt. Not only did the Pharaoh and Joseph give them the wagons and provisions but many other gifts. Benjamin was also given three hundred pieces of silver and five changes of clothing. To Israel they sent ten donkeys laden with the fine things of Egypt, ten female donkeys laden with corn, bread and meat. The brothers were sent on their way and to tell Israel all about Joseph being the governor over all of the land of Egypt. Israel did not believe and his heart was troubled. They told him the words of Joseph and when Israel saw the wagons that were sent to carry them back, he was overjoyed. Israel said, *"This is enough, Joseph my son is alive: I will go and see him before I die."*

Genesis 46

Israel made the journey to Egypt and stopped at Beersheba to offer a sacrifice to God. God spoke to Israel that night and again reiterated that he would make a great nation out of them and would be with them in Egypt. They went on to Egypt with their goods, cattle, and all of their kindred. Joseph and his family (his wife Asenath, sons Manasseh and Ephraim) went out to meet his family in Goshen. He met his father Israel and hugged him and wept. Israel said, *"Now that I have seen your face and know that you are alive I can die in peace."* Joseph said to all of them, *"I will go to the Pharaoh and tell him that all of my father's house has arrived in Goshen from Canaan. They are shepherds and they have brought all of their cattle to grow food for them."* This is what my people will tell the Pharaoh if he should ask, *"We are your servants, and we raise sheep and cattle."* They said this so the Egyptians would leave them alone because shepherding was an abomination to the Egyptians.

Genesis 47

The famine in Canaan was so bad that Joseph said to the Pharaoh, *"Now, therefore, we pray thee to let thy servants dwell there."* The Pharaoh answered, *"Your brethren have come unto thee, the land they are in is the best in Egypt so let them dwell there, if you know of any of your brethren among them who would tend my cattle make them rulers over them."* So Joseph brought his father Israel before the Pharaoh and Israel blessed him. The Pharaoh asked him his age and Israel answered, *"The years and days of my pilgrimage are one hundred and thirty years; few are evil of these days and years; a very few evil days and years have I experienced, as well as the life of my father*

Jacob Blessing the Children of Joseph

Rembrandt Harmensz. van Rijn - 1656

in the days of their pilgrimage." Israel again blessed the Pharaoh and left his presence. Joseph then gave his brethren the best of Egypt's land of Rameses as the Pharaoh had commanded. Joseph also gave them all enough food for survival since the famine in that part of their world was horrendous.

Joseph gathered the funds he had acquired in selling grain and brought it before Pharaoh. Everyone finally ran out of funds to purchase food, so Joseph collected their cattle, horses and donkeys: as payment for food. A year passed before the people had no possessions left and said, *"We have given all of our money, all of our livestock, and now all that is left is our bodies and the land we sojourn on. Purchase us and our land for food otherwise we will die."* Thus the Pharaoh ended up owning everything except the priests and their land. Pharaoh had decreed them an exemption. Joseph told the people, *"I have now bought you and your land but here is seed for you to sow the land. Upon harvest you will give Pharaoh one fifth of the harvest and keep four parts to yourselves."* The people said to Joseph, *"You have saved our lives so grace be unto you, and we will be Pharaoh's servants from now on."* This became the law of the land, except the priests which the Pharaoh did not own. Israel dwelt there until the age of one hundred forty seven years. His people prospered and grew and multiplied exceedingly. It came that Israel was about to die so he called for Joseph. He told Joseph that when he dies to take his bones and bury him with his people and not in the land of Egypt. Joseph made a covenant with his father that he would do this.

Genesis 48

Joseph took his two sons Manasseh and Ephraim with him to see his father before he died. When they arrived Israel told them that the Lord appeared to him in Luz (in Canaan) and blessed him, saying I will multiply your seed and will give them land as an everlasting possession. Your two sons are like Rueben and Simeon. On the way to Canaan, Rachel died, and I buried her in Ephrath which is Bethlehem. Israel asked Joseph who the two might be with him. Joseph answered by saying they are my sons. Israel asked Joseph to bring them to him so he could bless them. Israel's eyes were dim and could not really see them, so he hugged them and kissed them lovingly. He told Joseph he never expected to see him again, let alone his grandchildren. Joseph guided Israel's hand to his older son Manasseh's head but Isreal switched his hands. Joseph tried to change the way Israel was blessing his sons by saying place your right hand on Manasseh's head for he was the first born. Israel said, *"I know, I know,"* but he refused to do so and stated that the older brother will be great but his younger brother will be greater and become a multitude of nations. He also blessed Joseph saying, *"God was with Abraham and Isaac, and Isaac walked with God and this same god has walked with me and fed me all of my life up to this day"* (fed me here implies shepherd for the first time like a shepherd feeding his sheep). He said to Joseph, *"I will die but God will be with you and will again bring you unto the land of you fathers."*

Genesis 49

Israel next gathered all of his sons and asked all of them to listen to him. HE then either verbally blessed or prophesied over each one in turn:

- *"Ruben you are my first born, the beginning of my strength, but you went into your father's bed which defiled you."*
- *"Simeon and Levi, in your habitation you have turned out to be instruments of cruelty."*
- *"Judah is a lion's whelp and will be praised by his brethren, and unto him shall the gathering of the people be. The scepter shall not depart from him and his eyes will be red with wine and his teeth white with milk."*
- *"Zebulon will be master of the sea and ships, his boarders go unto Zidon."*
- *"Issachar is strong between two burdens, but will bear it and become a servant unto tribute."*
- *"Dan will make his people fall backwards (introducing idolatry into the Israel nation).*
- *Gad would fight the war like descendants of Ishmael and Esau, and others, but will prevail."*
- *"Asher would produce material prosperity and degeneracy."*
- Naphtali's tribe would characterized by both *"courage and eloquence"* (its great leader was Barak, i.e. Deborah and Barak in Judea).
- Joseph was the son through whom a significant fulfillment of prophecy happened (the exodus from Egypt) and his two sons (Manasseh and Ephraim) received separate prophecies and became tribes of Israel in their own right.

- *"Benjamin would be like a ravenous and successful wolf (from his tribe came King Saul and the apostle Paul)."*

From all of Israel (Jacob's) sons became the twelve tribes of Israel. When Israel finished commanding his sons he gathered his feet upon his bed and gave up his ghost (died) and was gathered unto his people.

Genesis 50

Joseph fell upon his father, wept and kissed him farewell and then instructed the physicians to embalm him as was the custom in Egypt. For forty days he was mourned. After morning Joseph told the Pharaoh that his father requested he be buried with his people. The Pharaoh told Joseph to proceed with his father's request. The families of Israel went with Joseph along with all of the royalty of Egypt. They went with horsemen and chariots, so the company that went to bury Israel was very great indeed. When the Canaanites saw this huge entourage they marveled and the name of the area became known as Abelmizraim which is beyond Jordan. Israel was laid in the cave of the field of Machpelah which Abraham purchased. Once the burial was completed Joseph, his brethren and family, plus the entire entourage returned to Egypt.

Joseph's brothers feared that with Israel now being dead that Joseph would turn upon them. When he heard this he wept in front of them and they were ashamed and bowed before him and said, *"We will be your servants."* Joseph said, *"Fear not for you meant evil against me but our God meant it for good to save as many of our people as possible. So fear not, I will nourish you and your children."* He comforted them and spoke very kindly to them. Joseph saw his son's Ephraim and Manasseh's children grow and held his grandson Machir's children upon his knees. Thus he lived a long and fruitful life. Joseph told his brothers, *"When I die God will surely visit you and bring you back out of this land unto the land he swore to be Abraham's, Isaac's and Israel's."* So Joseph took an oath with the children of Israel that they would carry his bones with them upon their departure from the land of Egypt. Joseph died at one hundred and ten years old, was embalmed, and laid into a coffin in Egypt. It was Joseph's faith in the future promises of God which placed him the "hall of fame" for faithful found in Hebrew chapter 11.

I'd like to end the book of Genesis with a few reflections upon the cosmic battle which has raged from the beginning of time and still rages within each one of us. At the beginning of the book of Genesis we are told that *"In the beginning God created."* Then we saw how sin and curse intervened, creating separation between God and humans. People were then separated into ethnic groups to slow the spread of evil. At the end of Genesis chapter eleven, we start to see the clarification of the plan by which God himself will become a human in order to take the penalty for sin upon himself. Abram and Sarai were the first in this line which would ultimately lead to Christ. They were renamed Abraham and Sarah by God. Out of them came Ishmael and Isaac, the two very different spiritual nations which have been opposing each other ever since. Do not be mislead into believing humans will solve all of our world problems. The spirit of our triune God is constantly working to direct people to accept the light (Jesus Christ our Lord). But until history is wrapped up and Christ returns the spirit of darkness will fight the spirit of light, causing the turmoil in this world. People will ultimately be separated into two groups – the sheep (those who have accepted the Lord Jesus as their Savior and Lord) and the goats (those who remain separated from their holy Maker because they have never made Jesus their Lord and Savior). Let the truth that is within you direct you (through love) from the darkness into the light. You cannot take anything with you when you leave this world except those whom you have helped into the light. At the end of this grand first book of the Bible, named Genesis, the people though whom God will ultimately provide a solution to mankind's sin problem are in the land of Egypt – brought there by God - through the faithfulness of Joseph.

part 3

Exodus to Deuteronomy
The Remaining Books of Moses

The Exodus

Exodus is the first book actually authored by Moses as Genesis was primarily a compilation of historical records. The latter part of Genesis was likely written by Jacob's sons with Moses tying it to the beginning of Exodus, using names instead of the word "generations." This book describes in detail the beginnings of Israel as a nation under the leadership of Moses. The high points are the Israelites deliverance from Egypt, law given out on Mt. Sinai, and their miraculous wandering in the wilderness for forty years. These were all acknowledged as real historical events until the time of Julius Wellhausen and other German scholars, which promoted what is known as the J, E, D, P theory in the 19th century - with the simultaneous spread of Darwinism in England. This theory, that believed there were multiple authors of the first books of the Bible and Moses may not even have been a real person. This type of rejection of the straightforward understanding of Scripture brought about liberal theology throughout Europe resulting in widespread rejection of the mosaic authorship of the Pentateuch and a subsequent disbelief in anything it had to say.

In spite of much subsequent evidence supporting the early records of Genesis, liberals continue to reject it as an accurate historical document, primarily because of their naturalistic commitment to evolution and millions of years for the age of the earth. They do this even though the mosaic authorship of the Pentateuch and its historical accuracy is fully accepted by later writers of both the Old and New Testaments. These writers certainly had better access to the facts involved than skeptics coming along 20 centuries later. God's Word, the Bible, will never be disproved because it is his truth inspired and protected through time by the one who is outside of time. So continue to believe it and not man's reinterpretation of it.

Four boxlike structures are prominent in the early chapters of the Bible. The first was Noah's ark – used to save mankind from the judgment of God. The second was the Reed ark (or basket) which floated Moses as a child on the river Nile and ultimately brought rescue to a people lost in bondage. The third was an "ark of the testimony" which is known as the "ark of the covenant" which contained the tablets of the law. The law reminded people that they were in need of forgiveness for they constantly broke the holy laws of God. This box had two cherubims and a mercy seat upon which God sat. The mercy seat was located between the cherubims. A fourth boxlike structure is also central to much that was to follow. This was the building of a tabernacle, or traveling house of worship, which housed the traveling ark of the covenant containing the laws of the Lord. Its purpose was to remind the Israelites of their commitment to God during their nomadic travels. The tabernacle was the home of God, where people would go to find forgiveness for their sins. I consider the last ark to be our Lord and Savior Jesus Christ who eliminates the need for the other structures and who will carry us to paradise through his actions on our behalf.

Other objects which are mentioned in these chapters are the Urim and Thummim - set in the high priest breastplate. These have been the objects of much speculation over the years. One translation of these names mean *"lights and perfection"*. They may have been in some way a medium of special divine guidance during the strategic period in God's plan for the people of Israel. Throughout Israel's history the nation willfully breaks God's covenant and God often had to discipline the people. Moses also had to discipline Israel because they were "stiff-necked people" (God's words). Aaron was the culprit by making the golden calf which was a common pagan symbol of fertility. Its worship was accompanied by promiscuous sexual activity. Moses asked God to forgive them. God said to Moses whosoever has sinned against me, him will I blot out of my Book of Life (unless that person has accepted Jesus Christ as his Lord and Savior and repented of his sins, then these sins are erased from your life - instead of your name being removed from the Book of Life). But we are getting ahead of the story. Exodus tells us of how the descendants of Jacob became a great nation with Moses as their leader. The Pharaoh at this time was concerned about the multiplication of the Israelite males, fearing they would join forces with other countries to destroy Egypt (evidently they were already being mistreated as slaves). The Pharaoh instructed all new born Israelite males to be cast into the river Nile and drowned - in order to slow the growth of the people. Population control, abortion, and infanticide are not new concepts!

Moses Found

Paolo Veronese - c. 1570-1575

Moses' mother devised a plan to save her son. She built a reed box (an ark) and placed it into the bulrushes of the Nile River where she knew the Pharaoh's daughter came to swim or bathe. Pharaoh's daughter spotted Moses and fell in love with him because he was such a beautiful baby. As he grew the Pharaoh also liked him and raised him as a son with all the education and power given to the elite in Egypt. Moses ultimately became the task master over the Hebrew slaves.

Eventually Moses learned that the people he was master over were his own people. He spotted another Egyptian taskmaster beating the Hebrew slaves, saw no other Egyptians watching, killed the man, and buried him in the sand. Thus the revered leader whom God ultimately chose to bring his people out of bondage…was a murderer. The next day two Hebrew slaves confronted him saying, *"You did wrong, who are you to judge over us, do you intend to kill us too?"* Moses realized that his crime was widely known. Pharaoh heard about it and sought to kill Moses so he fled far away to a distant land called to Midan. Moses was sitting by a well in Midan when a priest's seven daughters came to water their fathers flock. Moses stood up to help them. With his help they finished their task in record time. They returned to their father who asked how they had finished so rapidly and they told their father about Moses. The priest told his daughters to bring Moses home so he could eat bread with them. Moses liked what he saw so he dwelt with them. The priest gave him his daughter Zipporah to wed. She bore Moses a son who was named Gershom.

After many years in the wilderness the Pharaoh who wanted to kill Moses died. The Hebrew people cried to God about the labor and bondage. God heard their cries and remembered his covenant with Abraham, Isaac, and Jacob. God appeared miraculously to Moses in a flaming bush which was not consumed by this fire. Moses was completely surprised at this incident. God called to him out of this burning bush and Moses answered, *"Here I am."*

God told Moses, *"Take off your shoes because the place where you are standing is holy ground."* God told Moses He was the God of your father Abraham, Isaac and Jacob. Moses hid his face being afraid to look upon the Holy God. God then commanded Moses to lead his people out of Egypt. I will send you to the Pharaoh to tell him to *"Let my people go."*

Moses said to God, *"Who am I to go to the Pharaoh to let your children go?"*

God said, *"Moses don't, worry I will be with you. When you and my children come forth from Egypt, you all will serve me upon this mountain."*

Moses asked God, *"What is your name so I can tell the people?"* God answered by saying, *"I am that I am. Just tell them that I*

Moses at the Burning Bush

Rembrandt Harmensz. van Rijn - ca. 1655

am the God of their father Abraham, Isaac and Jacob. I also see what is now happening to you in the land of Egypt. I will bring you out of this land into the wilderness so you can sacrifice to the Lord your God. The Pharaoh may resist but I will stretch out my hand until he does."

Moses was still in doubt saying, *"They will not listen to me or believe that you appeared to me and besides I am slow of speech."*

God said, *"Haven't I made the man's mouth, or the dumb, deaf, or the seeing, or the blind?", "I am the Lord.", "Go and I will be with your mouth and teach you what to say."*

Moses was still very hesitant until the Lord asked him, *"Isn't Aaron, the Levite, your brother? He speaks very well and he will come to meet you and when he sees you his heart will be glad." "You will speak unto him and with both of your mouths I will teach you what to say." "Aaron will be your spokesmen unto the people." "So take this rod in your hand and with it thou shalt do signs."*

So Moses took the rod, or staff of God into his hands. God said you can do wonders with this staff before the Pharaoh to let my people go, but I will harden his heart so he will refuse. So tell the Pharaoh that the Lord says, *"Israel is my son, even my firstborn." "Let my sons go so they can serve me and if you refuse to let them go I will slay your sons, your firstborn."*

The Israelites accept Moses as their deliverer. They heard from Aaron that the Lord had visited them as well as Moses and was looking down upon their affliction. They all bowed their heads and worshipped their God. However, the Pharaoh rejects Moses. He said, *"Who is the Lord that I should let the Israelites go?"* The Pharaoh increased their brick making task by making them gather their own straw used in making the bricks, while requiring the same amount of production. This turned the Israelites against Aaron and Moses saying, *"The Pharaoh has done evil towards us and you have not delivered us from this situation."* God had to come to Moses to comfort him and assure him that they are a special

Moses' Journey into Egypt

Pietro Perugino - c. 1482

people set apart by God. They and all people who have faith in the triune God are all children of Abraham. But Moses was still not convinced and said, *"Lord, behold I am of uncircumcised lips, how will the Pharaoh listen to me?"*

The Lord spoke to Moses and Aaron. Go before the Pharaoh with your divining rod and perform miracles before him (when they did this Moses was 40 years old and Aaron was 43 years old). Aaron cast his rod on the floor before the Pharaoh and it became a live snake. Pharaoh was not impressed. He called his wise men before him and they cast down their rods which also became snakes (through the power of Satan's spirit). But Aaron's serpent ate up all the magician's serpents. This hardened the Pharaohs heart (like the Lord predicted) and the plagues began.

The first was changing the river Nile into blood. Next came the plague of frogs, and then came the plague of lice, followed by the fourth plague of flies. This plague finally convinced Pharaoh to let Moses, Aaron and the Israelites go to worship their Lord. Pharaoh did not want them to go very far to worship, but Moses insisted that they go at least three days journey to worship the Lord, but Pharaoh refused. Then came the fifth plague of pestilence upon the beasts. The sixth plague was boils on man and beast, with still no change in Pharaoh's heart. So along came the seventh plague of hail, followed by the eighth plague of locusts, the ninth plague of darkness and finally the tenth plague which was by far the worst of all - the death of every first born. Each of these plagues was specifically aimed at one of the gods whom the Egyptians worshipped. This showed the power of the true God of creation and the superior nature of the real living God over the false gods set up by mankind. The Lord was now ready to make the Pharaoh know the difference between God's people and the Egyptians. This was a classic foreshadowing of the battle between the children of light and the children of darkness. At this time Moses was given the instructions for the Passover because an angel of death was going to take every firstborn child but "pass over" those who obeyed his instructions. Moses told his people to take the blood of an unblemished lamb place it on each side and above the door post but not underneath, where it could be stepped upon. This formed a sort of cross over each family's door. This was a foreshadowing that Jesus would be called *"The Lamb of God"* and would someday come to shed his perfect unblemished blood so that eternal death would pass over those covered by his sacrifice.

The Lord came at midnight and passed over all of the Israelites homes sprinkled with the lamb's blood on the door posts, but killed all the first born males of the Egyptians including the Pharaoh's son. The Pharaoh woke up and saw as well as heard what the Lord had done to the Egyptians. He summoned Moses and Aaron that night and told them to gather the Israelites and take them into the wilderness to worship their Lord. The Lord had prepared them for this journey by having them eat the roasted lamb and unleavened bread. To this day the Israelites commemorate this occasion as the Passover feast. They not only took their dough (unleavened), their kneading troughs on their shoulders, but were given vast amounts of jewels, gold, silver and fine clothing from the Egyptians to take with them. They had become an aberration to the Egyptians who wanted nothing more than for them to leave the land.

There were six hundred thousand men on foot plus women and children riding on animals, plus their flocks and herds of cattle. They journeyed from Rameses to Succoth and left Egypt after being there four hundred and thirty years. Those that were circumcised were allowed to eat the Passover meal. Those servants and others uncircumcised who were traveling with them were forbidden to eat this meal. It was the month of Abib (March/April) that they came out of Egypt. Thus the Passover meal became a sacrificial ritual every year honoring the first born animal and human which belonged to God. Since the donkey was an unclean animal it could not be used as a sacrifice, so a lamb had to be substituted for the unclean animal and also for a human.   The reason being God lays claim to the first born ever since the Passover. This fact brought great comfort to me after my firstborn son died. Until I knew this from the ritual, I was very upset with God when he claimed my first born son at the age of twenty-six years, one month just before he was to graduate from electronic school and become married. But ultimately we all belong to God and if He deems it the right time to bring us home, who are we to argue.

By the strength of his hand the Lord brought the Israelites out of Egypt. Moses took the bones of Joseph with him remembering what Joseph had said to his brethren, *"Ye shall carry my bones away with you from Egypt, for our God will surely be with you."* They camped in Etham at the edge of the wilderness. The Lord went with them in a pillar of a cloud by day, and of fire by night, so they could travel day and night. They camped between Migdol and the Red Sea. God turned Pharaoh's heart again against the Israelites believing he could trap them between the wilderness and the Red Sea. He took six hundred chosen chariots and pursued the Israelites. When they saw that these chariots and Pharaoh's army were approaching them, they cried out unto the Lord. They also told Moses, *"Why did you lead us here into this entrapment? It would have been much better for us to stay in Egypt as slaves for the Pharaoh, then die here in the wilderness."* In spite of all the miracles they had not learned to trust the Lord.

The Crossing of the Red Sea

Cosimo Rosselli - 1481-82

Anyone who says they just need to see a miracle to believe in God, is fooling themselves. Any miracle can be explained away and soon forgotten - as the Israelites repeatedly did.

The Lord told Moses, speak to your people and tell them to go forward. Lift up your staff and stretch out your hand over the sea and divide it so you and the people can go across on dry land through the sea. The Lord caused the waters to part permitting all of the Israelites and their entourage to cross with a huge wall of water on each side of them. They crossed and the Egyptians came after them. Moses lifted up his staff and stretched his hand for the waters to come together again resulting in the drowning all of the Egyptians plus the chariots and captains in the process. Those who try to explain this miracle by natural causes (such as a shallow spot in the sea or a strong wind) are ignoring what the text says about a *"wall of water on each side"* and the collapsing wall drowning the entire Egyptian army.

The Israelites (and many others) saw the great work which the Lord did upon the Egyptians. This made the people fear and believe in the Lord as well as Moses. The Israelites sang unto Moses (the first song recorded in scripture) and unto the Lord. This song of Moses is referred to in revelation 15:3 where Moses' song is combined with the "Song of the lamb" at the glassy sea in the heavenly temple. Moses brought them from the Red Sea into the wilderness of Shur. After three days in the wilderness they found no water. They came to Marah (meaning bitter) where the water was bitter and undrinkable. They asked Moses again, *"What shall we drink?"* Moses cried unto the Lord and the Lord showed him a tree whose bark caused the water to become drinkable. Moses told the people that if they would listen to the Lord and keep his statues they would never have problems too great to overcome. He did not promise no problems in life – just that the Lord will take us through those trials.

At Elim they came upon twelve wells of water and forty palm trees where they camped. They came into the wilderness on the second month after their departure from Egypt. Everyone began to grumble against Moses and Aaron. Having no food they said, *"At least we could eat while in Egypt, but now we are in the wilderness and will die of hunger."* The Lord told Moses he would rain manna from heaven to provide for the people. Not only did the Lord provide manna but quails into their whole camp. They gathered enough to eat each day but on the sixth day they gathered twice as much to last through the next day which became the Sabbath day (or day of rest) which had been observed since creation week. Some tried to gather on the seventh day but found none. The Lord asked Moses a rhetorical question to reveal the disobedience of the people, *"Why don't the people observe my commandments and laws?"*

The people left the wilderness of sin and arrived in Rephidim. No water was found there. They chided Moses for water and Moses cried to the Lord saying these people thirst and

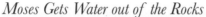

Moses Gets Water out of the Rocks

Jan Havicksz. Steen - c. 1660

they are ready to stone me. The Lord told Moses to take his staff along with the elders to Horeb, where you will find a rock to smite with your staff and out of it will pour water. Moses named this place Meribah because of the Israelites lack of faith saying, *"Can't you see and understand that the Lord is with you?"*

Later the Amalek arrived to fight with the Israelites in Rephidim. Moses told Joshua that he would stand on the hill with his staff in hand and Joshua should take men and go fight.

He said that God would be with them (the Amalek's were cruel people being descendents of Esau). Whenever his arms were up Joshua would advance and when Moses dropped his arms they were pushed back. Moses arms grew weary and had to be held up by Aaron and Hur so his staff stayed up. The Lord told Moses to write this in his book as a memorial to Joshua's victory over the Amalek's. Moses built an altar to the Lord at the site of this victory and named it Jehovahnissi which means *"The Lord is my banner."*

At this point Jethro, Moses father-in-law heard about Moses and how the Lord had helped him bring all of the Israelites out of Egypt. Jethro brought Moses wife, Zipporah, and his two sons, Gershom and Eliezer, to Moses. Moses met them with a bow of courtesy, kissed them, and invited them into his tent. Moses explained how the Lord provided their miraculous escape from the Pharaoh. Jethro took a burnt offering to the Lord along with sacrifices while Aaron and all of the Israelite elders came to eat bread with Moses and his father-in-law. Jethro watched while Moses spent day after day acting as judge for all of the Israelites - executing the statutes and the laws of God all day. Jethro told Moses that this is not good, *"You will wear away from all of the stress."* Listen to me and I will tell you what to do, *"Select men you can trust with God's word and teach them God's ordinance and make them heads over the people of Israel, some ruling over thousands, some over hundreds, others over fifty and some even over tens. So they judged the people over all of the seasons bringing only the very difficult ones for Moses and settling the smaller matters themselves."* After that Moses' father-in-law departed and went back into his own land.

On the third month of their journey they came into the wilderness of Sinai, where they camped. Moses climbed to the top of Mount Sinai as the Lord commanded. The Lord told Moses to tell his people that he the Lord delivered them out of Egypt on eagle's wings. Therefore, they should obey my voice and keep my covenant, *"For you shall be my special people above all, because this Earth is mine. You will be unto me a kingdom of priests and a holy nation."* This is when Moses called all of the elders together and told them what the Lord said. They and all the people accepted this special responsibility saying, *"All that the Lord has spoken we accept and will do."*

The Lord came upon Mount Sinai to speak to the people after they had sanctified themselves. The Lord descended upon Mount Sinai in fire and smoke and the whole mountain shook. When the trumpet sounded, Moses called upon God, who responded by calling Moses to come on up climb up the

Moses on Mount Sinai

mountain again. He told Moses to tell the people not to break any of the commandments of the Lord or they would perish. Moses did as he was instructed. Aaron and Moses went up and the Lord gave them Ten Commandments – revealing the very character of God and instructing people about how to live in peace with God and each other. The fourth Commandment destroys any possibility that evolution could someday explain our existence.

Jacques de Letin

"For in six days the Lord made Heaven and Earth, the sea, and all that is in them, and rested the seventh day: wherefore the Lord blessed the Sabbath day, and hallowed it." God did not need rest on this day because our Lord never tires over his watch on us but set this pattern up for our benefit. This is the only one of the Ten Commandments which comes with a justification attached. Thus we honor God and rest on the seventh day because everything was made in six literal normal days.

The people saw and heard all of this, but asked Moses to speak for them before God because they were so afraid of the Lord. Moses said, *"Fear not, for God has come to prove that his fear may be before you that you will not sin."* The Lord said, *"Now the children of Israel have seen that I have talked to you from Heaven, so make no false gods, make an altar of Earth and sacrifice burnt offerings of peace from thy sheep and oxen in all places where I record my name and I will be with you and bless you. Build me an altar of stone but lift not your tool upon it otherwise you will pollute it, nor go up its steps unto it or thy nakedness will be discovered thereon."* Next the Lord set the rights of persons, as well as again ordaining capital punishment for crimes against parents. This area of the Bible clearly indicates these rights and where the term, *"Eye for eye, tooth for tooth, hand for hand, and foot for foot"* comes from. Next is the right of property, then stealing and trespassing. Then the book of Exodus describes the proper conduct of people, describes our responsibility to bring the "first fruits" of all our wealth unto Him. We also learn about justice and mercy – being instructed to never oppress the poor or the stranger since, *"you were all strangers in the land of Egypt."* The Lord finally instructed the Israelites to till the ground for six years and let it rest the seventh year in the same way they were instructed to work six days and honor the Lord your God on the seventh - making it a Sabbath day. Once again this is a direct tie to the reality of a recent literal creation.

The three feasts for the Israelites came next - the feast of unleavened bread, the feast of harvest (first fruits) and the feast of the ingathering (which comes in the end of the year). On these three occasions all the males in Israel were to gather before the Lord.

Their conduct toward their enemies was explained next. They were instructed not to serve any other Gods, *"For if you do it will be a snare unto you."* Moses told the people what the Lord had said and all answered, *"We will do what the Lord has instructed."* This covenant of the Lord was sealed with blood. The young men offered a burnt offering and peace offering unto the Lord. Moses placed the blood of the sacrificial animals into basins and sprinkled half of it upon the altar. He took the book of the covenant and read it to all of the people and they said, *"All that the Lord said we will do and be obedient to this covenant"*. Moses took the remainder of the blood, sprinkled it upon the people saying, *"This is the blood of the covenant which the Lord has made with you concerning all these words."*

Moses was instructed to take Aaron, Nadab, and Abihu plus the seventy elders and go to worship afar off, but only Moses came into the presence of the Lord. Moses wrote all these covenants down, rose up early, and built an altar unto the Lord, placing twelve pillars representing the twelve tribes of Israel. Moses went unto Mount Sinai as instructed by the Lord for forty days and nights. A cloud covered it six days and on the seventh day the Lord spoke unto Moses in glory like a devouring fire - which all of the children of Israel could see. The Lord instructed Moses about the purpose of the tabernacle, the ark of the covenant, the table of the showbread, the golden candle sticks, the curtains of linen, the purpose of the boards and sockets, the outer veil, the brass altar, the court of the tabernacle, the oil for the lamp, the priests garments, the ephod, the breastplate (with Urim and Thummim) the robe of the Ephod, the holy crown, and finally the priests' coats. Moses was then instructed how the priests were to be hallowed and their continual offering. The instructions included specific commands concerning the altar of incense, the ransom money, the laver of brass, the anointing of oil, the incense with the instructions for building the tabernacle. All of these specific commands involved symbolism pointing to the coming of Christ as the one who would ultimately become <u>the sacrifice covering our sins.</u>

Near the end of the book of Exodus the Lord repeated the command about the importance of the Sabbath saying, *"For in six days the Lord made the heavens and the Earth and rested on the seventh...".*

Moses Showing the Ten Commandments

Gustave Dore - 1865

Then the two tablets are given to Moses by God ending the communing on Mount Sinai, with these two stones giving us the commandments of God written with his finger. Isn't it any wonder it took Moses forty days and nights to write down all of this information?

Sadly, when Moses came down from Mount Sinai, the Israelites were worshipping a golden calf instead of God. They had given their gold and silver jewelry to Aaron so he could form the golden calf from it. When Moses came down from Mount Sinai and saw this worshipping of idols he was so angry he smashed the stone tablets God had given with the commandments. Moses then ground the golden calf to dust and made the Israelites eat it. God told Moses he was going to destroy the Israelites for their disobedience but Moses asked for God's mercy and once again God relented and spared them even though they did not deserve His mercy.

The tabernacle was constructed and pitched outside of their camping area. When the people learned that the Lord considered them "stiff-necked" they mourned and did not put on their ornaments. Moses went into the tabernacle to speak to God, while the Israelites stood at their tent doors to watch. God said he will show Moses the way to the Promised Land. God shows Moses his glory but Moses is not allowed to see God's face but only his back. At this point God tells Moses to carve two more stone tablets like the ones which were broken. God instructed Moses to come in the morning by himself, atop Mount Sinai with the two tablets. God again wrote the Ten Commandments upon them.

Moses asked God to accept the stiff-necked people and pardon their iniquity, taking them as an inheritance. God said they must destroy the inhabitant's altars, images, and cut down the groves of the Amorites, Canaanites, Hittites, Perizzites, Hivites, and Jebusites because He is *"a jealous God"*, and wanted no other Gods. This is as true today as 4000 years ago. It is for our own good that no desires can compete with our commitment to the Lord. The people were to keep the feast of the Passover (unleavened bread) because God brought them out of Egypt in the month of Abib. They were to also keep the feasts of the first fruits, wheat, harvest, and the ingathering at the year's end - appearing before God at the tabernacle three times a year.

When Moses came down from Mount Sinai his face literally gleamed as if lighted from within. When Aaron and the Israelites saw this they were afraid to come near Moses. Moses covered his face with a veil so they would not be afraid; he then told the Israelites what God expected of them. The glory of the

Lord was with them in the tabernacle. The cloud of glory had been with them day and night ever since they left Egypt.

Unfortunately when they came to the land God had promised them, only two of ten in the advance scouting party believed God was capable of giving them the land. Majority never determines truth yet the people believed the eight rather than the two (who had faith in God). As punishment for not trusting the Lord every adult except those two scouts – Joshua and Caleb, ended up dying from forty years of wandering in the wilderness outside of their promised inheritance land. Lack of trust in the Lord always results in death! Yet God stayed with them the forty years of unique divine power and provisions. None of God's miracles in Exodus can be explained in terms of normal processes of nature.

Leviticus

Leviticus is the third book of Moses. This book continues with the narrative of Exodus, where the glory of God is speaking to Moses out of the tabernacle of God. Central to this book is the design and construction of God's house- the tabernacle. As with the other books of the Pentateuch, liberal critics allege that Leviticus was written long after Moses and even after the return of the Israelites from their Babylonian exile. This book, however, claims that the Lord spoke all these things directly to Moses. The entire outlook and all of the incidental references (the sacrifices in the tabernacle, the allusions to the wilderness, references to the camp, etc.) speak only of the Exodus period and never of the later temple worship.

A very remarkable phenomenon is that the largest percentage of this book contains verbatim quotations from God himself. We believe that the entire Bible is divinely inspired, but the particular method of inspiration varies widely from book to book. However, in this particular book, large portions are essentially divinely dictated.

The major emphases include the various types of offerings ordained by God along with repeated affirmations of the holiness of God. The consecrated duties of the priests are described as well as the various ritual laws. The dietary laws for God's covenant people are found in the eleventh chapter, and

: note omitted

the provision for the great Day of Atonement is the sixteenth chapter. The feasts of the Lord are described in the twenty-third chapter. There is a remarkable prophetic sequence in the twenty-sixth chapter. This book closes with the following summary: *"These are the commandments which the Lord commanded Moses for the children of Israel on Mount Sinai."* With Moses asserting that over ninety percent of its verses are dictated by God, I ask you, *"Is there anything too hard for our Lord?"* (Gen. 18:14).

In order to make true atonement for sin (like the shedding of first blood in the garden of Eden when God killed an animal to cover Adam and Eve with clothing from an animal skin), the blood of an innocent substitute must be shed. This practice anticipates the eventual offering of the sinless blood of the "Lamb of God" as a once-for-all offering for the sin of humankind.

Numbers

This book of the Pentateuch gets its name from the two "numberings" of the children of Israel. The first census was taken soon after their escape from Egypt. The second census occurred at the nearing end of their forty year wandering in the wilderness as this new generation was preparing to enter the Promised Land. Chapters five through twenty-five recount the number of experiences of the Israelites in their wilderness wanderings along with additional instructions given by God to Moses during that time. This section of the book ends with the Israelites remarkable encounters with the false prophet Balaam (chapters twenty-two through twenty-five). After the second census, the last ten

Amminadab

Stained Glass Window - 12th century

chapters (twenty-seven through thirty-six) give the Israelites
further instructions concerning offerings and feast days, as well
as other events occurring as Israel was getting ready to invade
Canaan.

Conservative Biblical scholars believe the Israelites' wanderings occurred during the period from approximately 1447
B.C. to 1407 B.C., assuming that the chronology from earlier
chapters is totally correct. There is some valid disagreement
over exact dates. This places this period of earth history
approximately 3500 years ago – long before the time of the
classical Greek empire. Numbers records events from the
wilderness period. Despite the obvious mosaic authorship (this
book contains at least eighty statements to the effect that the
"Lord spoke unto Moses"), liberal theologians (those who do
not consider the clear straightforward statements of the Bible as
authoritative) still allege that most of this book was written by
priests living after the Babylonian Exile. There is certainly no
proof for such an assumption. Internal evidences from the book
itself, as well as correlation with much archaeological evidence
about this period, fit well with the wilderness period as the
setting for this book.

Deuteronomy

This is the last book of Moses, this title means "second
law" (from the Greek deuteros and nomos, meaning "second
and law"). This name is derived from the fact that this book
(Chapter five verses six through twenty-one) reiterates the Ten
Commandments as well as many of the other mosaic laws as
first given in Exodus, Leviticus, and Numbers. The earlier laws
are also enlarged and also applied to in various ways. It is as
if the last thing Moses wanted to leave with his people was an
absolute command to live holy lives and obey the Lord. He had
seen the nature of human beings and knew they would stray
from the truth and wanted to repeat yet again the importance of
obedience.   This book can also be considered Moses farewell
speech which reviews the history of the nation and their escape
from Egypt. It includes three components, delivered at different
times and places (Deu.1:5, 4:46, and 29:1), but all at various
locations in the land of Moab just east of the Jordan River.

Israel had been in the wilderness for almost forty years and finally preparing to enter into the Promised Land. Moses would not be able to go with them, but would die in the land of Moab after viewing Canaan from afar (Deu. 34:1-6) and having turned over the leadership to Joshua (Deu. 31:7, 14 and 27:18-23).

This book is frequently cited in the New Testament. It contains Israel's great statement of monotheistic faith (Deu. 6:4-6) as well as Christ's "greatest" commandment (Deu. 6:5). Jesus chose words from this book to turn back the three temptations of Satan (Deu. 6:13, 16 and 8:3). Remarkable prophecies of both blessings and curses on Israel are found in chapters twenty-eight and twenty-nine. The song of Moses is also recorded in chapter thirty-two and his final prophetic blessings on each tribe (except Simeon's) is recorded in chapter thirty-three.

The fact that Moses wrote this book can be found in frequently claims (Deu. 31:9, 24) and has all the evidence from both internal and external examination. Jesus often quoted from it, accepting the mosaic authorship (see Mat. 19:8 citing Deu.24:1-4). Moses authorship was accepted by all authorities ancient and modern, Jewish and Christian. Yet the rise of evolutionary-based "higher criticism" which has its foundation in the rejection of the straightforward statements of Genesis also rejected Moses as having written this book. Since that time most liberal scholars have denied that Moses wrote Deuteronomy, but they cannot agree as to when and by whom it was written. Some have attributed it to the time of King David, others to the revival under King Josiah, and others to the post-exile period. Such speculation is mere fantasy, deriving from the evolutionary prejudices of such skeptical theologians.

Beyond any reasonable questions, Moses is the author of this book written at a time very near the end of his life. There is no doubt that Joshua wrote the account of Moses death (see chapter thirty-four) and possibly other editorial explanations. Joshua probably added these to the mosaic document after Moses died and then continued to preserve all of the mosaic writing by placing them in the Ark of the Covenant as described in chapter thirty-one verses twenty-four through twenty-six.

part 4

Joshua to Ester
The Historical Books of Israel

The Book of Joshua

This book immediately follows the Pentateuch, chronologically as well as sequentially. Its main theme is that obedience allows people to take possession of the land given to them and disobedience causes them to lose the land. Some liberal scholars view Joshua and also the rest of the Pentateuch as one book they call the Hexateuch, alleging that all these six books were written and edited many centuries after the time of either Moses or Joshua, in an attempt to fabricate a history that would unify and encourage a fragmented nation. There is little support for this position.

The name "Joshua" is equivalent to "Jesus" - both meaning "Jehovah is savior." Joshua was the successor to Moses who led the children of Israel across the Jordan to conquer and inhabit the promised land of Canaan. There is little doubt that Joshua himself wrote this book, with the exception of the account of his own death and certain explanatory editorial comments that were added later. The final chapter is an affirmation by Joshua that he wrote the words of this book and then added them to the books of the law left by Moses (Jos. 24:26). Both the internal evidence and uniform tradition agree that Joshua was the author.

Joshua Fights Amalek

Nicolas Poussin - ca. 1625

There has been no indisputable evidence from archeology which would disprove any aspect of the book's historicity or divine inspiration. The New Testament book of Hebrews refers to its accounts as true history (Heb. 4:8; 11:30-31). Rahab (2:6) is also recognized in Mathew 1:5 as a real historical person, in fact, in the ancestry of Joseph, the legal father of Jesus. The divine inspiration of Joshua 1:5 is further indicated by its quotation from Hebrews 13:5.

The account of Joshua records two of the most remarkable miracles in history - signaling God's determination to fulfill his ancient promise to Abraham in giving the land of Canaan to the descendants of Abraham. The heavy walls of Jericho at the entrance to this Promised Land fell down flat in response to the trumpets of the priests and the shout of the people (Jos. 6:15-20). Then the sun itself "stood still in the midst of heaven" (Jos. 10:13) to enable Joshua's army to rout the confederation of Amorites that otherwise might have eventually turned them back.

On the basis of the reference in Hebrews 4:8, Joshua, leading the people of God into the Promised Land, can even be considered as a type of the greater "Joshua" our Lord Jesus leading his own people to eternal life in the new Jerusalem. What a great future we all have to look forward to.

The Book of Judges

This book is the second of what are called the historical books of the Bible, immediately following Joshua. This name, Judges, refers to the gifted men (plus one women - Deborah) whom God raised up to lead and govern Israel between the times of Joshua and Samuel. All together fourteen of these judges were named in the book including Deborah and Barak, who served as sort of co-judges, but not including Eli and Samuel, who judged Israel later.

The authorship of this book is unknown although the most likely candidate is believed to be Samuel. The period involved is at least three-hundred years, it is probable that records were kept by a number of writers, then later compiled and edited by Samuel after the period of Judges had passed. This eventual editor/writer was, of course, guided by the Holy Spirit in such a way that the book was divinely inspired and is inherently correct.

The chronology of this book has been somewhat controversial. The total length of both the Judges rule and the intermittent periods of captivity was about four hundred and ten years, but this turns out to be too great to be in accord with other chronological data (see Kings 6:1). Many writers, therefore, assume that some of the listed judges may have governed different regions of Israel at the same time. A few writers, however, believe that there may be significant gaps in the records and the total period could have been much longer. The archaeological evidence is also uncertain, but it should be remembered that methods of dating ancient events (i.e. pottery dating, radiocarbon dating, tree-ring dating etc.,) are often contradictory and are based on some very questionable assumptions. Furthermore, even though the numbers in the original writing of Scripture were inherently correct as divinely inspired, transitional scribe errors in copying

older manuscripts possibly occurred. Thus one must be very
cautious in ascribing specific dates to the various incidents, not
only in Judges but also in all of the earlier books of the Old
Testament. However, over 99% of the oldest manuscripts of
the Bible agree perfectly with modern translations and the few
controversial differences are of little or no significance to any
basic Christian doctrine. This is a remarkable confirmation
of God's hand of protection over his written word over more
than 4000 years of history since the flood.

The main characteristics of this segment of Israel's history
seems to have been cyclic repetition of national fellowship
with God, then apostasy, followed by captivity and finally
repentance, deliverance and restored fellowship. One of
the sadist indictments of the people during such periods of
apostasy is contained in the very last verse of Judges: *"every man
did that which was right in his own eyes"* (Jud. 21:25; 17:6; and Det.
12:8). This statement could be written today about America
and the Western world. Without an absolute standard of
morality (outside of human intellect) – and that is what God's
Word claims to be - every society will ultimately decay into
moral sewage. In America we seem to be in this situation
today since the foundational belief in the Bible as a source
of truth has been rejected. This started with the rejection of
Genesis as a document revealing the truth about our origin;
and as stated in the first chapter of the book of Romans, this
rejection of God as literal creator has inevitable lead to the
current situation in the Western world with the Bible's moral
guidance being rejected, and especially the last book – The
Revelation.

Despite a few uncertainties of the authorship and its
chronology, as well as the frequent periods of apostasy and
servitude, the historicity of the records in Judges has been confirmed in the New Testament as stated in Acts 13:19-21 and
Hebrews 11:32. Today we are witnesses to the same sort of
moral apostate conditions but our outlook should be positive
because of the imminent second coming of our Lord.

The Book of Ruth

This is one of the books in the Bible featuring a specific woman. The other such book will come later and is called the book of Esther. Ruth was a Moabite whose people were perpetual enemies of God's chosen people - the Israelites. Amazingly, Ruth actually appears in the genealogical ancestry of Jesus (see Math. 1:5) by marrying Boaz, the great-grandfather of King David (Ruth 4:21-22). The author of this book is unknown and its final edited form must date back from

Boaz

Michelangelo Buonarroti - fresco 1508-1512

the time of David (Ruth 4:7 & 4:18-22). It is probably that Samuel or David himself may have been the final, inspired author.

The historical setting of this book appears to be in the time of Judges (Ruth 1:1) but whether earlier or later in this

period is uncertain. The Jewish historian Josephus says that
Ruth lived at the time of Eli when Samuel was young, which
would correlate with the implication that she was David's
great-grandmother (Ruth 4:21-22). However, if Salmon was
both the husband of Rahab, and the Father of Boaz (Ruth
4:21 & Matt. 1:5)...that would make Rahab a mother-in-law
of Ruth. This places Ruth early in the period of Judges.
Since that period lasted three or possibly four hundred fifty
years (see Acts 13:20), it seems that there must be a significant
gap somewhere in this genealogy. If Josephus was right (and
he should be, being closer to this time than we are) that gap
is most likely between Salmon and Boaz, thus Salmon begat
Boaz in the ancestral sense rather than the immediate sense.

   The story of Ruth is beautiful and inspiring. Even in the
turbulent time of the Judges, God will providentially look out
after his people and is concerned about individuals in other
nations. God made all people and they are precious to him.
Ruth also provides a striking type of Christ in the person of
Boaz, who became the "Kinsman-redeemer for Ruth" (Ruth
4:1-12). He brought her into the family of God's people by
paying the price for her redemption, just as our Lord Jesus
purchased us all with the price of his shed blood (see Eph. 1:7)
in order that we all can become part of the eternal family of
God by accepting him as our sacrificial lamb. This book is a
beautiful story of what our God's love can and will do.

The First Book of Samuel

   These two books were originally only one book in the
ancient Hebrew Canon, but became two in the Greek
Septuagint translation of the Old Testament. Samuel may be
considered the last of the judges (1 Sam. 7:15). When Samuel
attempted to appoint two sons as judges to succeed himself (1
Sam. 8:3), they proved to be unworthy. The people demanded
a king. This book is therefore significant in describing Israel's
transition from a theocracy to a monarchy.

   In addition to being a judge, Samuel was also a priest (1
Sam. 7:9; 13:11-14) and prophet (1 Sam. 3:20). He probably
was the founder of the so-called "school of prophets; which
proved so important in Judah and Israel for centuries to come

(1 Sam. 19:20). He was never king of Israel, but did have the privilege of being used by God to anoint as king first (Saul) and the second king (David).

Samuel wrote the first twenty-four chapters of this book himself, but he could not have written much more than this, as events of 1 Samuel chapters twenty-five through thirty-one occurred after his death (1 Sam. 25:1). It is possible that the prophets Nathan, followed by Gad, who were probably trained by Samuel, wrote these later chapters - as well as perhaps all of 2 Samuel, (see first Samuel chapter 29:29). The final author or editor is unknown, however, and it may be that whoever it was simply used the earlier records of Samuel, Nathan and Gad in compiling their own account under divine inspiration. Even 1 Samuel could not have been put into its final form until at least the days of Rehoboam, for the kingdom had already been divided by the time this was done (1 Sam. 27:6).

Just as Moses had placed his books of the law in the Ark of the Covenant to be preserved there (see De. 31:24-26), so did Joshua (see Chron. 27:24). It is at least possible that these records were kept by Nathan or Gad, both of whom outlived David. In any case, there is reason to believe that we have actual eyewitness accounts of the events described in both 1 Samuel and 2 Samuel. This was an extremely important period for Israel (like our world economy today), marking both the great revival under Samuel after the dark period of the later judges - especially Eli. This period also contains the transition of the United Kingdom under David and Solomon, the time of Israel's pinnacle of greatness. This book describes in detail how lowly David, the least of the sons of Nathan, was chosen by God to be the leader of the Israelites. One of the great lessons of this book is that God is more concerned with our heart than our appearance. Our actions will always follow our hearts. David was described as a man after God's own heart. His desire was to please God and even when he "blew it" he would return to God in repentance (just as we should).

The Second Book of Samuel

This second book deals almost entirely with the reign of David. It records the establishment of Israel's (eventually Judah's) capital in Jerusalem, and also the great messianic promise to David (2 Sam. 5:6-9; 7:12-16). The account of his great sin concerning Uriah and Bathsheba is found in 2 Samuel chapters eleven and twelve, and the rebellion of Absalom in 2 Samuel chapters fifteen through eighteen. The book closes with the account of his sin and punishment concerning his self-willed census-taking (see chapter 24), near the end of his reign.

It is worth noting that the two books of Samuel and the two books of Kings were called in the Septuagint translation the four "Books of Kings". It was not until the sixteenth century that the present terminology for the four books began to be used. In view of the subject matter in 2 Samuel, it could have been well called the Book of David. As such, it is one of the key books in the Old Testament. David was thirty years old when he began to reign, and he reigned for forty years.

Bathing Bathsheba

Artemisia Gentileschi - 1650

David had trouble over the Ark of the Covenant. The first time the Ark was handled wrongly (see 1 Chron. 13:1-14) and chapter six. David then rejoices over the ark of the Lord. Dancing with such joy and fervor that his cloths flew off. When Saul's daughter Michael chastised David for this indiscretion, it was her, not David, who was disciplined by the Lord. The Lord is honored if we worship and obey him with everything within us – even if we do occasionally "slip up" in the process.

David is not allowed to build an earthly tabernacle to the Lord but is promised an eternal house (1 Chron. 17:1-2 and 17:3-15). Chapter eleven covers David's adulterous affair with Bathsheba which ended with his murdering her husband. This can happen to any male who is tempted by a lovely woman. To think we are above such actions is to fool ourselves. Jesus clarified this point by saying, *"If thou commit adultery in thy mind (dwelling upon a female with lust), it is as though thou has committed the act."* Men must always bear this in mind and work to control their actions – starting with their thoughts.

In chapter twenty-one we are again told about the giants in Gath, some with even six fingers and six toes, David's nephew slew one of them. There were four who were born to the giant in Gath who were killed by David and his servants. Many believe this was a continuation of the pollution of the human race which started back in Genesis chapter 5 with the Nephilim. Although David was not allowed to build God's temple because he was a man of war, he did purchase the land from Araunah upon which the temple of Solomon would eventually be built.

The First Book of Kings

This book originally was known as the third book of Kings until first and second Samuel came into the picture. It continues the life of David starting with the rebellion of Adonijah, the coronation of Solomon, the death of David, the details of Solomon's reign, featured by the building and dedication of the temple in Jerusalem, and the sad fall of Solomon, his death and then the tragedy of the divided kingdom, followed the rebellion of Jeroboam against Rehoboam. These events are recounted in the central chapters of this book, with the rest devoted to the conflicts of Judah and Israel with each other and other nations. Of special significance is the story of the prophet Elijah, in his interaction with King Ahab and the prophets of Baal. The book continues through the reign of Jehoshaphat in Judah (the great grandson of Rehoboam, son of Solomon) and Ahaziah in Israel (the seventh king of Israel following Jeroboam). The total period covered by this book is approximately one-hundred and twenty-six years, from accession of Solomon to the reign of Jehoram.

No one knows who wrote this book. The final editor used various sources with which to compile the inspired record which we now have. Jewish tradition indicates that the prophet Jeremiah was the man responsible for the final compilation and editing of both first and second Kings. The Jews had considered both Samuel and Kings to be included in the books of the prophets (as distinct from law and the Psalms). The books of Kings are filled with many prophetic insights, so it could well be true that the original record, as well as the final editing, were produced by one or more of the prophets. In this book we learn about King Solomon, his foolish marriage, him seeking wisdom from God, and then upon receiving it, how he demonstrates the use of it.

Before we move on to the second book of Kings, I need to explain the division of Israel into two separate nations - Israel (the northern kingdom) and Judah (the southern kingdom with the city of Jerusalem). Solomon's son King Rehoboam foolishly burdened his people with unjust taxation demands. The United States is moving in this same direction. In 930 B.C. the ten northern tribes rebelled against Rehoboam, splitting Israel into two kingdoms. The ten northern tribes united to form the kingdom of Israel under King Jeroboam, while the two remaining tribes, Judah and Benjamin, formed the southern kingdom of Judah under King Rehoboam. Each Kingdom was ruled by a separate line of kings - a few of them righteous but most of them evil. God sent his prophets to Israel and Judah repeatedly to warn the people of his promised judgment for their continued unfaithfulness, but the warnings fell largely on deaf ears. In spite of rare periods of spiritual revival, the prevailing trend in both kingdoms was toward great apostasy and idolatry. This should be a great warning for this great nation, to heed this same warning before it is too late.

In 721 B.C. the northern kingdom was captured by Assyria and almost everyone who was not killed was exiled there (now known as modern day Iraq and Iran). Judah remained for approximately 130 more years before being conquered by prince Nebuchadnezzar of Babylon. God at this point removed his divine presence from their temple.

The Second Book of Kings

The second book of Kings continues the history of Judah and Israel (Israel became known as the northern kingdom and Judah became known as the southern kingdom which contained the city of Jerusalem). Like first Kings this second book was probably compiled from the records of the earlier prophets by Jeremiah or one of the later prophets of Judah.

The ministries of two prophets of God - Elijah and Elisha - constituted the dominant subject of the first third of this book. The history of Israel is sad in the extreme, with one ungodly king after another leading the people away from God, until finally the Assyrians destroyed their land and carried the people off into captivity. The last king of Israel was Hosea (see chapter 17).

There were some believers and faithful servants of God in the northern kingdom during all those years of spiritual decline and apostasy. The most notable were the prophets of Elijah and Elisha, but two of the prophets of the biblical Canon had ministries primarily in Israel. Hosea's initial ministry to Israel was during the long reign of Jeroboam, but it evidently continued even beyond Israel's exile into Assyria (see Hosea 1:1). The prophet Amos was a contemporary of Hosea who also ministered especially in the northern kingdom of Israel (sometimes called Ephraim).

In Judah, several of the kings were God-fearing men - Hezekiah and Josiah in particular led in great national revivals. Prophets whose ministry was centered in Judah were (more or less chronological order) – Obadiah, Joel, Isaiah, Micah, Nahum, Habakkuk, Zephaniah, and Jeremiah. Isaiah, in the days of Ahaz and Hezekiah; and Jeremiah, during the last days of the kingdom under Josiah; and the kings who briefly followed him, had especially significant influence on kings and the nation as a whole.

No doubt because of the influence of these prophets, and the several God-fearing kings of Judah, God allowed Judah to remain in the land for about one-hundred and thirty years after Israel had been carried away to Assyria. Eventually, however, even Judah became so wicked and apostate, especially under her final kings (Jehoiakim, Jeconiah, and Zedekiah) that God sent Nebuchadnezzar and the Armies of Babylon to destroy Jerusalem with its temple and to carry the king and all of the leaders into exile and captivity in Babylon.

There were other godly prophets and priests in both Israel and Judah, of course, besides those whose prophecies have been preserved in the Bible. Some among these, no doubt, were the original writers of the records which are now recorded and incorporated in the books of Kings. The last of them was Jeremiah, quite possibly the man who compiled and edited all of these earlier documents into their present, divinely inspired form.

Before we move away from Kings, I want to note that our loving God gave his children what they had requested – earthly kings to rule over them. They should have been satisfied to have God himself as their only king – the revealer of truth and knowledge. For the most part their kings were an extremely bad influence upon the nation. Even two of the most famous kings - David and Solomon – failed miserably. Both of these kings allowed females to draw them away from their devotion to God and to satisfy the desire of their flesh. Satan in the Garden of Eden enticed the human race to eat from the tree of knowledge clearly revealed to humans the choice between good (God) or evil (Satan). From this has grown today's theological compromise. There is a constant temptation to accommodate pagan beliefs or practices in the worship and service of the true God of creation. This satanic device is used in every age, including our own.

One of the greatest problems in modern Christianity – in fact, probably the most serious of all – is the widespread capitulation of our Christian intellectuals to the ancient pagan system of evolutionary pantheism, as they attempt to equate "creation" with "evolution" and the literal days of creation week with the evolutionary ages of historical bible-denying geologists. Thus they become false prophets as our Lord said we would have in these later days. So I continue to pray "please come soon Lord Jesus" so our days will not become like the days of Noah just before the worldwide flood.

Before we move into Chronicles, I need to make one more observation. In going back to Genesis 5:24, Enoch (who had served God as a great prophet in a time of deep apostasy), was taken into heaven (that is the "third heaven", where God's throne is located, see Hebrews 11:5 also) without dying, but evidently no one had actually observed his ascension to heaven as was seen when Elijah was taken directly to heaven without dying. Enoch's ministry was to mankind during the midpoint between Abraham to Christ. Elijah was taken up in a fiery tornado that seemed to surround a fiery horse-drawn chariot as he went up until he was out of Elisha's sight. It is thought by some, including myself, that Elijah and Enoch have been both supernaturally preserved in heaven ever since that time in their natural bodies. Yet Scripture says that it is appointed to all men one time to die. Thus I also believe that God will send them back to Jerusalem in these later days to be the two witnesses who will be proclaiming Christ during the anti-Christ regime talked about in the book of Revelation. They will then be martyred for this cause as all of the world watches via worldwide satellite TV. This will be a true physical death like the one Jesus experienced. My youngest daughter believes (through premonition) that she will be martyred with these two witnesses. I pray to the Lord that she will be raptured before this happens.

Elijah's Ascension

Gustave Dore - 1865

The Two Books of Chronicles

Like the two books of Samuel and the two books of Kings, these two books were originally one book. First Chronicles deals mainly with the reign of David, substantially paralleling but abbreviating Samuels account. Second Chronicles begins with the reign of Solomon and continues through Judah's entire history to the time of the Babylonian invasion and exile, thus paralleling the two books of Kings. However, Chronicles essentially ignores the corresponding history of the northern kingdom.

These books date from the post-exiled period because some of the genealogies in the first nine chapters extend into that period. In the final two verses of 2 Chronicles it speaks of the decree of Cyrus authorizing the rebuilding of the temple. This suggests that Ezra the scribe probably was the final editor and author. In fact there exists significant evidence that Chronicles was originally one book with Ezra and Nehemiah. Ezra's authorship is not unquestioned, but it seems reasonable and is confirmed by almost unanimous Jewish tradition.

The books of Chronicles were written long after Samuel and Kings, and the Chronicler no doubt had these two (or four) books to select from in developing his account. There were also numerous other ancient documents and records available, some of which are actually mentioned in the Bible. An example is the mention of the writings of the prophets Nathan and Gad (29:29). In Second Chronicles the authors mention "The book of the Kings of Judah" (2 Chronicles. 16:11); *"The book of the kings of Israel"* (2 Chron. 20:34); and the *"Book of the kings of Judah and Israel"* (2 Chron. 25:26). There are other numerous sources listed, some twenty in all. Since all of these ancient documents are lost, there is no way of knowing which of them were used by Ezra (or whoever the Chronicles may have been recorded by). He undoubtedly used Samuel and Kings, since many sections in Chronicles are almost exact quotations (11:1-3 with 2Sam. 5:1-3).

A natural question why such duplication is necessary when the four books of Samuel and Kings were already available. From the viewpoint of the returning exiles however, it was important for them to have a document establishing their ties with their founding fathers, and with their continuing role in the plan of God for his chosen people, and with the eventual messianic kingdom. Therefore, the detailed genealogies and the strong emphasis on David and the Davidic line leading ultimately to the Messiah are again recorded in these books. This theme not only explains why certain events were duplicated but why certain new records were added and why there were many omissions. As far as the latter are concerned (the events of Saul's reign, the history of the northern kingdom, David's sin and Absalom rebellion, Solomon's moral decline in his later years) - these were records of failure and rebellion which had no ultimate bearing on that great theme which the Chronicler needed to emphasize. The ultimate apostasy of Judah and her exile, of course, had to be included to explain the situation in which the returning exiles now found themselves.

Just as there is duplication in the four gospels of the New Testament, so also there is duplication between the books of Chronicles and the books of Samuel and Kings. Nevertheless, in both cases, the superficial amount of duplication merely serves as conformation of the historicity of the nation. This duplication gives a greater in-depth understanding of God's great plan. The ancient scribes were very meticulous and copy errors are few and far between. We can have confidence that Chronicles, as well as all other books of the Bible, have been preserved substantially intact. The present Authorized Version still gives overwhelming evidence of inherent inspiration, even in such books as Chronicles.

The Book of Ezra

Ezra is identified as *"a ready scribe in the law of Moses"* (7:6). He is also called *"Ezra the priest"* (7:11) and a descendent of *"Eleazar, the son of Aaron the chief priest"* (7:1-5). Although not all conservative scholars agree, it is reasonably certain that Ezra himself wrote this book, as well as the two books of Chronicles. The last two verses of Second Chronicles are almost the same as the first two verses of Ezra, the author thereby indicating that the one was intended as a continuation of the other.

The combined accounts of Ezra and Nehemiah, along with other Prophetic books of Haggar and Zechariah, tell the story of the returning remnant of Jews after their seventy year captivity in Babylon, undertaking to rebuild the city of Jerusalem, its walls, and the temple. It is interesting that just as the exile from the land took place in three separate stages (2 Chron. 36:5-20), so the return took place in three stages. First, the returning remnant was led by Zerubbabel, as governor, together with Joshua the high priest. They rebuilt the temple and reestablished worship. This story is recounted in the first six chapters of Ezra. It was during this period of eighty years, that the prophets Haggar and Zachariah exercised their ministry, encouraging the people to continue the work in spite of much opposition. The decree of the Persian emperor Cyrus, in about 536 B.C., initiated this phase. The second group came under Ezra in about 458 B.C. following a decree by Artaxerxes that gave Ezra both political and religious authority over Jerusalem, as well as financing to furnish the rebuilt temple and to restore it to some measure of its former dignity and beauty. The third wave came after another decree by Artaxerxes in about 445 B.C. given to Nehemiah, whose main commission was to rebuild the walls of the city. This mission is described in the book of Nehemiah.

Two sections of Ezra (4:8-6:18; 7:12-26) were written in Aramaic. They were essentially letters and decrees, and presumably Ezra simply copied them as they were, without translating them into Hebrew (Aramaic was the diplomatic language of the near east at this time). It is also worth noting that one of the Apocryphal books, One Esdras, purports to have been written by Ezra. However, it contains a number of contradictions with the Canonical book of Ezra, with the latter rather obviously providing the true record.

The Book of Nehemiah

This book, along with Ezra, was once considered to be one book because Ezra and Nehemiah were contemporaries in the post-exile Jerusalem. There is much in common between these two books. In fact, many of the ancient scribes believe that Ezra actually wrote the first chapters of Nehemiah, but the internal evidence strongly favors Nehemiah as the author.

Nehemiah was a high official in the court of Artaxerxes, who was king of Persia. As a Jew, however, he was greatly concerned about the reestablishment of Jerusalem and the temple back in Israel. Approximately fourteen years after Ezra received his decree from King Artaxerxes, Nehemiah obtained another decree from the same king giving him the authority to rebuild the wall around the city. This decree was prophesied by Daniel as the beginning of the "Seventy Weeks" in Daniel's famous prediction of the coming of the Messiah (Da. 9:24-27).

Under Nehemiah's dynamic leadership, the walls were quickly rebuilt, despite opposition from the previous inhabitants of the land. Under Ezra's spiritual leadership, and Nehemiah's governmental leadership, the remnant nation experienced a significant religious revival, though it never again completely gained its independence. The reading of the law in the rebuilt temple caused weeping, as the people realized their failures. Nevertheless God had preserved them, as he had promised, and this new beginning was a time for thankful rejoicing. The term, *"the joy of the Lord"* occurs elsewhere only in Matthew 25:21,23, where the Lord rewards his faithful servants with the invitation to *"enter thou into the joy of thy Lord"*. This term was first used as people re-established their relationship with God in Nehemiah 8:10.

The Book of Esther

This is the second Biblical book centered on a woman - the first one being Ruth. This is the only book of the Bible with no mention of God anywhere in its chapters; although the providential hand of God is marvelously evident throughout this book.

The setting is in the court of the great Persian emperor Xerxes (same as the Biblical Ahasuerus), where Esther had been queen, despite her Jewish background. The events described apparently took place partially before and partially after the time of Xerxes' ill-fated attempted invasion of Greece.

The authorship of Esther is uncertain. A number of scholars think that Ezra may have written it, since the time corresponds to that of Ezra, and both were associated with the Persian court. Many others ascribe it to Mordeci,

Ester and Mordecai

Arent de Gelder - 1685

Esther's older cousin and mentor. For some unclear reason, the author made considerable effort to keep his account free of any mention of God, prayer, or other religious matters. Presumably, this was because there was considerable anti-Semitic feeling in Persia at the time, very likely because of the attempted human genocide and the Jews' bloody vengeance in return. Nevertheless, one senses the strong faith Esther and Mordecai, as well as the remarkable sequence of providential ways in which God, behind the scenes, was preserving his chosen people.

Although no direct confirmation has been found of Haman's attempted genocide and the other events described in the book of Esther, all that is known about the times, places and people in the book is consistent with all known data from

ancient history and archaeology. There is no valid reason to
doubt the historical accuracy of the book of Esther.

The annual feast of Purim of the Jews was established by
Esther and Mordecai as two days "of feasting and joy, and of
sending portions one to another, and gifts to the poor" (9:22),
in commemoration of their remarkable deliverance from their
imminent annihilation as a people and nation. The name
Purim, meaning "lots", seems strange for a holiday, but it was
based on Haman's evil device to "Cast pur", that is, the lot...
to consume them, and to destroy them (3:7, 9:24) when the
month Adar (i.e. February-March) came. This decision by lots
(possibly specially marked stones), rather than helping Haman,
turned out to have been so ordered by the Lord that a wait of
almost a full year was required. It thus provided ample time
for all events to be set in motion which would finally bring
Haman's evil scheme back on his own head.

Esther is Introduced to Ahasuerus

Rembrandt Harmensz. van Rijn - ca. 1655

part 5

Job to Song of Solomon
Books of Wisdom & Worship

The Book of Job

This book tests the faith of a man named Job. We get a rare look into the spiritual realm as Satan asks God's permission to test the faith of this man. This is spiritual lesson number one. Nothing, absolutely nothing happens without God's permission and Satan is only given limited freedom to test us. God gives permission as long as Satan did not destroy Job's life. Job went through hell on earth losing his wealth, family and health. At the same time his supposedly good friends were giving him the wrong advice. I am certain many of us have gone through trials and tribulations because we have trusted advice from the wrong source rather than putting all of our trust in our triune God and His word.

The first eleven chapters of Genesis were apparently written by Adam, Noah, the sons of Noah, Terah, and eventually edited by Moses. We know this because they contain details which could only have been observed or known by people alive during this early period of earth history. There is actual no such thing as prehistoric times. Apart from Genesis

the book of Job is probably the oldest book in the Bible
because it describes events prior to the time of Abraham and
makes reference to both dinosaurs and the ice age – both of
which were most prevalent on earth immediately following
the great flood. It contains more references to creation, the
flood, and other primeval events than any book of the Bible
except Genesis and provides more insight into the age-long
conflict between God and Satan than almost any other book.
Remarkably, it also contains more modern scientific insights
than any other book of the Bible.

Uniform Jewish tradition ascribed the origin of the book
of Job to Moses and also accepted it as part of the true Canon
of scripture. This
ascription seems
quite reasonable if
Moses is regarded
as the editor and
original sponsor
of Job's book.
Undoubtedly Job
himself was the
original author (see
19:23-24), writing
down his memoirs,
so to speak, after
his restoration to
health and prosperity.
Moses most likely
came into posses-
sion of Job's record
during his forty-year
exile from Egypt in
the land of Midan
(not very far from
Job's own homeland
in Uz), and quickly

Job and his False Comforters

Jean Fouquet - 1452-60

recognized its great importance. He likely edited it for the
benefit of his own contemporaries. This was probably similar

to the way that he compiled and organized the ancient records through which he has given to us in the Book of Genesis.

Job, according to God's own testimony, was the most righteous and Godly man in the world, at least up to that time (Job 1:8 & 2:3). It is confirmed in Ezekiel 14:14, 20 and in James 5:11 that he was a real historical person, and not just a fictional character in a great dramatic poem. St. Paul also quotes from Job 5:13 in 1 Corinthians 3:19.

Job evidently lived about or before the time of Abraham. It is significant that despite the prevalent ancient tradition of Moses' connection with the book, the book of Job nowhere mentions the mosaic laws or even the children of Israel. It clearly was written well before the time of Jacob (or Israel, as God named him). Throughout the land of Uz, Job was considered *"The greatest of all men of the east"* (Job 1:3) and *"dwelt as a king in the army"* (Job 29:25). The antiquity of Job is further indicated by the fact that he probably lived at least two-hundred years (Job 42:16) - longer even than Abraham (Genesis 25:7). Less genetic mistakes upon earlier humans and the deterioration of conditions on earth following the great flood have both been given as possible reasons for the reduction in lifetimes for humans after the flood. In any case the farther removed we have become from the original creation, the shorter our lifetimes have become - settling to around 80 years at the time of David and not changing much since that time. Original lifetimes after the fall of 800 or more years are a distant, lost memory. Job lived much closer to the time of the great flood than Abraham and other Bible patriarchs so he had a very long life indeed.

Job's book is considered the masterpiece of literature, even by those who reject its historicity and divine inspiration. Its pervasive theme is the mystery of the suffering in a world created by a righteous and omnipotent God. Though this may be the theme of the book, that is not its purpose, for the book never answers that question. Even God, in his remarkable four-chapter monologue (Job 38 thru 41), never mentions the question at all. Rather, God emphasizes the vital importance of the doctrine of special creation and the sovereign right of the creator to use and test mankind (made in his image) as he wills. God is never unjust and never capricious, and we must simply rest and rejoice in this fact through our faith. It is by focusing on God, His creation, and His awesome power and nature, rather than our own problems and circumstances, which will get us through the problems which surround us.

God Answers Job

William Blake - c. 1804

It is also fascinating to note that at the end of the account Job is given double of everything he had before the tragedy struck him **except his children** - where he is given the same number. In actuality he was also given double the children because his original children, even though killed, are only dead in this physical reality. Job would see them again after death. Thus the number of Job's children, was in reality, also doubled! What a comfort to those who have lost their children. We will be reunited with them someday in heaven as long as they have been cleansed by the blood of The Lamb.

Psalms

This is the longest book of the Bible, occupying a key position in the plan of our triune God and his instruction to his people. It is fitting that Psalms is in the center of the Bible and the longest book in the bible because it is all about worshipping our Maker. It contains the Bibles longest chapter (119) and also the shortest (117). There are numerous references to the primeval past and even more to the prophetic future, being especially rich in statements concerning the coming Messiah. It is undoubtedly the favorite Bible book of multitudes of believers because of its poignant insights into our needs and God's provisions...our sorrows and the joy of the Lord... all of it still relevant to God's people in every age.

Many of the Psalms have inscriptions indicating their human authors. Thus David is listed as author of seventy-three Psalms, Asaph of twelve, with one Psalm each attributed to Moses, Heman, and Ethan. That leaves sixty-two of them anonymous. However, three of these psalms (2, 72 & 95) are also elsewhere identified as David's. Thus the "The sweet singer of Israel", the man who was called a *"man with a heart after God"* (who was also a murderer!!!), wrote at least half of the psalms. The book of Psalms can be subdivided internally into five "books" (Chapters 1-41; 42-72; 73-89; 90-106; 107-145), plus a five chapter (146-150) "epilogue." The significance of this particular grouping is not clear, though there might be an implied tie of some kind to the five books of the Pentateuch. However, it is noteworthy that each of the five books ends with a grand doxology (41:13; 72:19; 89:52; 106:48; 145:21). Then, each of the five psalms in the epilogue is a great psalm of praise, both beginning and ending with "hallelujah!", meaning "praise the Lord"! The last verse commands: "Let everything that has breath praise the Lord. Praise ye the Lord" (150:6).

The book of psalms has been called "The hallelujah book" and also "The book of praises of Israel." However, there are very few psalms (67; 100; 133) which contain only a note of praise and nothing else. Almost all the psalms sing of sorrow and suffering, opposition and persecution – yet always in the context of God's redeeming love and the believer's overcoming faith, leading finally to the everlasting praise of our creator and savior.

There are also many keen scientific insights scattered through the psalms, as well as many evidences of remarkable structure. Sometimes the structures are intentional, as in the "acrostic" psalms, where each successive line begins with the successive letter in the Hebrew alphabet. At other times they seem unintentional, except as woven into the structure by the Holy Spirit - as special evidence of divine inspiration and spiritual testimony.

Unlike other books of the Bible (in which the chapter and verse divisions were inserted only by medieval scholars) the chapters and verses of the book of psalms seem to have

been impressed upon by the poetic
structure of each psalm from the
very moment of their divine inspiration (Psalm 22:22 is an example
- also known as the Psalm of the
cross).

    Although the immediate context
of the Psalms is in relation to the
nation Israel and her worship, they
are clearly an infinitely precious
resource for believers of every
time and place. I cannot begin
to cover the beauty, wisdom, and
significance of all the knowledge
imparted to us through the Psalms.
Therefore, I will just present the
text of perhaps the most well
known Psalm as representative of
the significance of the entire book.
In my opinion, the most popular
Psalm is the twenty-third one, the
Psalm of the "good shepherd".

King Solomon

Duccio di Buoninsegna - 1308-11

    The Lord is my shepherd; I shall not want.

    He maketh me to lie down in green pastures: He leadeth me beside the still waters.

    He restoreth my soul: he leadeth me in the path of righteousness for his name's sake.

    Yea, though I walk through the valley of the shadow of death, I will fear no evil: for thou art with me; thy rod and thy staff they comfort me.

    Thou preparest a table before me in the presence of mine enemies: thou anointest my head with oil; my cup runneth over.

    Surely goodness and mercy shall follow me all the days of my life: and I will dwell in the house of the Lord forever.

    I have heard this Psalm read at many Christian funerals
and each time I pray that they died in Christ, because if
they didn't, regardless of the Psalms intent, it will not give

the person the results the Psalm states. Only those who die in Christ will dwell in the house of the Lord. Furthermore, just as this Psalm states, death is merely a dark valley…a shadow…we must all pass through. There is definitely an eternity waiting for us on the other side. The question each of us must answer is whether we desire to spend that eternity in the presence of our Maker and Shepherd, or spend eternity separated from Him.

Proverbs

This book has been ascribed to King Solomon, who *"spoke three thousand proverbs: and his songs were a thousand and five"* (1 Kings 4:32). Even though the first verse of Proverbs claims Solomon's authorship for the book, it is probable that he collected many of them from various sources (see Ecc. 12:9). The last two chapters were apparently written by two men named Agur and Lemuel, respectively (Pro. 30:1; 31:1). Whether Solomon wrote or collected them, their present form is rightly attributed to Solomon (Pro. 10:1; 25:1), with the present form of the book possibly organized by the servants of King Hezekiah (Pro. 25:1). There is also a possibility that certain sections were written by a school of servants known as *"the wise"* (Pro. 22:17 and 24:23).

The book has been organized in several distinct sections. The first seven verses constitute an introductory statement of purpose, involving the impartation of eleven aspects of God's mind to the learner (wisdom, instruction, understanding, justice, judgment, equity, subtlety, knowledge, discretion, learning and wise counsel). Following this is a section – from Proverbs 1:8 through 9:18– seventeen lessons begin with statements of *"my son"* or *"ye children"* (1:8,10,15; 2:1; 3:1,11,21; 4:1,10,20; 5:1, 7; 6:1,20; 7:1,24; 8:32). Prominent in these lessons, and throughout most of the book, is the contrast between two symbolic women, *"wisdom"* and *"folly"*, of the *"virtuous women"* and the *"strange (or foreign) women."*

The collection of 375 proverbs from Proverbs 10:1 through Proverbs 22:16 have no specific theme for continuity. Each proverb is an independent pithy saying with no relation to context, often consisting of a couplet of either supporting or contrasting assertions. The sections written, or collected, by *"the wise"* (22:17-24:22; 24:23-34) also consist of wise sayings on many subjects, but in most cases continuity is retained through several verses. Another set of isolated independent proverbs in Proverbs 25-29, under the heading of *"proverbs of Solomon, which the men of Hezekiah King of Judah copied out"* (25:1). Hezekiah was King of Judah about 300 years after Solomon; thus the book of proverbs did not assume its final form until long after Solomon's day.

Finally there are the last two chapters, credited to Augur and Lemuel, respectively. Neither of these men are otherwise identified though there have been many speculations. Proverbs 30 is a striking chapter with many quotable verses. The testimony of Lemuel in Proverbs 31 includes the famous acrostic poem (31:10-31) on the *"virtuous women."*

The wisdom of proverbs, although seeming disjointed, contribute to the full, rich life of a true redeemed follower of God. Each one deserves thoughtful study and careful meditation. Taken as a whole Proverbs show that God is directly concerned with every detail of our lives.

Ecclesiastes

Ecclesiastes is the Greek Septuagint word equivalent to the Hebrew word translated *"the preacher"* (Ecc. 1:1). The writer claims to be *"the son of David, King in Jerusalem"*. In other words Solomon claims to be the author of this book and this is the traditional view of both Jews and Christians. However, many scholars, including a number of conservatives, have argued that while the purported writer is Solomon the book was actually written long after his day. Nevertheless, there is good reason to believe that Solomon wrote it himself, probably in his old age, in his later years. He was certainly capable of giving us the wise counsel contained within this book if anyone ever could – especially concerning the *"vanity"* of a life centered *"under the sun,"* in contrast to a life dedicated to the spiritual realm *"above the sun."* The deep purpose of Ecclesiastes seems to be convincing younger people of the futility of worldly learning, riches and pleasures, as ends unto themselves. One goal is to exhort readers to *"remember now thy creator in the days of thy youth"* (Ecc. 12:1).

The book contains a number of striking scientific insights (Ecc. 1:4-7; 3:14-15; 11:5), as well as powerful theological truths (Ecc. 3:11; 4:13; 7:20; 11:1). There are numerous individual wise sayings, similar in style to the book of Proverbs. Indeed, the preacher claims to have *"sought out [truth], and set in order many proverbs"* (Ecc. 12:9). Despite the book's enigmatic questioning of a future life, the preacher never doubts the existence of God or a future judgment. It is assumed throughout the writing that God exists and there will be a judgment for our actions.

The book's basics question is whether ANY human endeavor is sufficient to bring a worthy purpose to life. And this theme is explored by a man who has had it all and done it all! If there is any man in all of human history capable of answering this question it was Soloman. Soloman's legacy included unimaginable wealth, power, intelligence, entertainment pursuits, and sexual satisfaction (with over 500 "wives"). Yet this man came to the conclusion, after having experienced EVERYTHING this world had to offer, that the true purpose of life could be summed up with one statement – obeying God. In sum, the book of Ecclesiastes, despite its superficial pessimism, is actually a fascinating treasure of deeper spiritual insights and faith.

The Song of Solomon

Like Ecclesiastes, the Song of Solomon (also known as "song of songs" and "canticles," meaning "songs" in Latin) is fascinating and enigmatic, providing striking testimonial to the unique, wide-ranging wisdom of Solomon. Like the other two books, it claims to be from Solomon (Song. 1:1). Solomon was said to have written over a thousand songs (1 Kings 4:32), but this was his "song of songs." The Song of Solomon is unique in being written like a play, with different persons speaking (or singing) as the theme develops. The different speakers are Solomon himself, Solomon's bride (called Shulamite in the song), the daughters of Jerusalem, and the brothers of the bride.

This book was written early in Solomon's reign, long before his many wives turned his life away from devotion to his first love. Although there have been a number of interpretations of this book, the most obvious interpretation is no interpretation at all. That is, it is simply what is purports to be – a romantic love poem describing the love of a young Solomon and a Shulamite maiden who became his first bride.

There is nothing unseemly about a book of the Bible depicting the beauties of pure courtship and marital love. Yet it is so explicit in its language that young Jews were not allowed to read the book until they reached their teenage years. The union of male and female in holy matrimony is intrinsic to the creation itself (Gen. 2:24-25). In this sense, the narrative of the song can be considered as an idyllic picture of courtship and marriage that might apply, with varying details, to all true love and permanent marriage as ordained by God. Why anyone would chose another lifestyle (divorce, multiple partners, infidelity, or homosexuality) is a testimony to the sinful nature of mankind and does not make any common sense.

In secondary sense, the account may also be considered as a type of the love Christ and his church "the bride of Christ" (Eph. 5:22-33; Rev. 21:2; 22:17). This analogy should not be pressed too far, as the book should primarily be studied in accord with its own clear intent, that of describing and honoring the God – ordained union of man and woman in true love and marriage.

It seems almost certain that the young bride whom Solomon loved so passionately was Naamah, who is said to have been mother of his son Rehoboam (2 Chron. 12:13). Rehoboam had been born a year before Solomon became King, for Solomon reigned forty years, whereas Rehoboam was forty-one years old when he became King (2 Chron. 9:30). Solomon was almost certainly less than twenty years old when he himself became King, and Rehoboam was already a year old at that time. Therefore, Naamah was evidently *"the wife of his youth"* and the bride eulogized so beautifully in his song of songs.

part 6

Isaiah to Malichi
Books of the Prophets

Isaiah

Although Isaiah was not chronologically the first of the prophets, he is universally considered the "prince of the prophets". This is not only because of the length of his prophecy (although the prophecy of Jeremiah is slightly longer) but because of the majesty and beauty of his themes and the many prophetic pictures of the coming messianic kingdom. The fifty-third chapter of Isaiah contains probably the clearest and fullest exposition of the sacrificial suffering of Christ in submission for our sins to be found anywhere in the Bible - including the New Testament. Yet it was written down over 500 years before his birth! The book begins with a painful depiction of the sinful lost condition of the people, but ends in the triumphant creation of the new heavens and new earth.

Isaiah was a prophet in Judah, serving under several Kings in his long career – Uzziah, Jothan, Ahaz, and Hezekiah (Isa. 1:1). His most influential ministry was under King Hezekiah, who led the nation in its greatest spiritual revival since the days of David and Solomon. Critics, as usual, have viciously attacked the book of Isaiah, insisting that there were at least two "Isaiah's" – one who wrote chapters 1-39, the other, chapters 40-66. Some have even suggested three or four authors. The ostensible reason for the unwarranted assertion of multiple Isaiahs is the need to discredit God's Word as being capable of being understood in a straight-forward way. There are several

The Prophet Isaiah

James Tissot - ca. 1888

literary styles used in this book of the Bible that to assume that this proves multiple author-ship is like saying that a poet is incapable writing anything but poetry.. Critics ignore the fact, however, that the two different styles relate to the two different themes of the two sections, not to mention the fact that there are far more similarities than differences that can be found in the two sections.

The real reason however, for the two Isaiah's notion is that the second division contains many remarkable prophecies that were later fulfilled – for example, the naming of the Persian emperor Cyrus a century and a half in advance of his coming to the throne (Isa. 45:1-4). Skeptical theologians are unwilling to believe that

God can supernaturally reveal the future to his divinely called and prepared prophets, and so, must assume that the last part of Isaiah was written by an unknown writer living among the exiles in Babylon after Cyrus had conquered the city.

This criticism not only accuses the prophet of deception but also defies the uniform belief of both Jews and Christians all through the centuries. Furthermore, both the apostles and Jesus himself frequently quote from both sections of Isaiah, always

attributing them to Isaiah with no suggestion that they were
quoting from two different men. For example, Jesus attributes
his quotation of Isaiah 40:3 to "the prophet Isaiah" (Math
3:3) and his quote of Isaiah 6:9-10 to "Isaiah the prophet"
(John 12:38-41). The oldest manuscript of Isaiah is found in
the Dead Sea scrolls, dated about 100 B.C., and this gives no
indication whatsoever that it was not written by the same man.
The same is true of the Greek Septuagint translation of the
Old Testament. In fact, all genuine historical evidence agrees
on the unity of Isaiah. Therefore, there is no reason to doubt
the authenticity of the entire book.

Isaiah's book is a marvelous document containing history
and prophecy, clearly pointing forward to the coming Messiah
and the fulfillment of all God's purposes for both Israel and his
whole creation of this world.

Jeremiah

This is our second major prophet. Jeremiah, the last of the
pre-exile prophets (i.e. prior to the Jews being in Babylon). He
is often called "the weeping prophet" because of his impas-
sioned pleas to his people and their leaders to repent, repeatedly
warning them of severe judgment and exile if they did not.
America is in the same situation today. Founded as a very godly
nation, it is slipping into total apostasy. The Bible has lost all
credibility to those outside of the church and disaster is just
around the corner because we as a nation have rejected the
only possible source of moral absolutes. We cannot say that we
haven't been warned and most will ultimately, but too late, have
to admit that God basically has said, "I told you so."

The prophetic ministry of Jeremiah extended over some 40
or more years, under the reigns of Judah's last five Kings Josiah,
Jehoahaz, Hehoiakim, Jehoiachin (or Jeconiah, also Coniah),
and Zedekiah. Josiah was a godly king who had led his people
in a great revival (though it turned out to be somewhat superficial and short-lived). Jehoahaz, Jehoiakim, and Zedekiah were
sons of Josiah, whereas Jehoiachin was a son of Jehoiakim.
Each of these four kings "Did that which was evil in the sight
of the Lord," according to all that his fathers had done" (see 2
Kings 23:32,37; 24:9,19). The reforms of Josiah were forgotten

soon after his death, with both kings and the people quickly returning to the pagan ways of the 55-year reign of wicked King Manasseh, grandfather of Josiah. Amon, Josiah's father, reigned only two years before he was assassinated (see 2 Kings 21:1-2, 19-20, 23). Most of Jeremiah's warnings were necessitated by the evil ways of these last four kings, including his great

The Prophet Jeremiah

Michelangelo Buonarroti - fresco 1508-1512

prophecy of the impending 70-year captivity in Babylon (Jer. 25:9-12; 29:10 & 2 Ch. 36:21).

As to Jeremiah himself, he was not of the priestly tribe of Levi, but son of Hilkiah the priest, born in Anathoth. This city, assigned by Joshua to the tribe of Benjamin (Jos. 21:18), was probably the same as modern Anata, about three miles northeast of Jerusalem. Jeremiah was called to his prophetic ministry in the 13th year of Josiah's reign (1:2). Josiah was king for 18 more years, whereas the last four kings only ruled a total of 22 or 23 years. Actually Jeremiah continued his ministry for an uncertain additional period in Egypt, among those of the people that fled there while most of the Jews were being carried away to Babylon (Jer. 43-44). No one knows for certain when or where he died, although tradition has it that he was slain by the Jewish refugees in Egypt to whom he was still preaching.

The times of Jeremiah were tumultuous. The great nations of the time – Egypt, Assyria, and Babylonia were fighting for supremacy and Judah was often involved, situated in their midst. Similar fighting in the region continues to this day. Eventually Babylon, under Nebuchadnezzar, defeated Assyria. Egypt retreated resulting in Babylon becoming the world's dominant empire for some 50 years. All of these nations were very wicked themselves, so that even though God used them to punish Israel and Judah, their time for judgment was also coming. Among the prophecies of Jeremiah were the ultimate judgment of Egypt, Philstia, Tyre, Moab, Ammon, Edom, Syria, Hazor, Elam, and especially Babylon. Assyria had already been defeated by this time (Jer. 46-51).

There are many wonderful messianic prophecies in Jeremiah, promising ultimate deliverance and restoration of Israel in the future messianic kingdom (we saw one of these fulfilled in May of 1948 when the Jews returned to their homeland after almost 2000 years in exile – an event unheard of in all human history). In Jeremiah is the first revelation of the coming "New Covenant" which God would make with Israel as well as Judah (31:31-37) and which would eventually encompass all of God's people in every age (see He. 8:6-10:25).

It is obvious that God still has his guiding hand of protection over his people (the Jews). I strongly disagree with those who declare that God has forgotten his first covenant with the Israelites and who claim that the church has taken over this first covenant. In reality, since the time of Christ, we are living in an age were Jews have been "grafted" into God's kingdom (called messianic Jews). But a time will come when the spirit-filled church will be removed and the Jews will awaken to realize, en-mass, that their Messiah has already come a first time to make atonement for the sins of all mankind. He is also coming a second time (I believe soon!) to wrap up world history and end the 6000 + year old battle between evil and good. What kind of a God would Jehovah be if he gave an unconditional promise to make the Israelites his people and then withdraw this promise because of their performance? It would violate the very character of who God is – infinite in trustworthiness, mercy, and justice.

Lamentations

This short book of the Old Testament is included among what many call the Major Prophets because it is actually sort of an appendix to the book of its author Jeremiah. Three of its five chapters being "how"? (Hebrew Eykah, which was the Hebrew title of the book). In context, the title is essential answering the question of "why the distruction of God's people happened." Jeremiah wrote his "lamentations" after he witnessed the destruction of Jerusalem and its temple by Nebuchadnezzar and his Babylonian armies. Though he had predicted it, it was a great sorrow for him to see his prophecies actually come to pass. He wanted to make sure people under-stood why these things were happening.

Each chapter is composed as an acrostic poem, with 22 verses corresponding to the 22 letters of the Hebrew alphabet, each verse beginning with its successively appropriate letter of the alphabet. The middle chapter has 66 verses - devoting three verses to each letter. Because of this unique structure and style, some authorities say that someone other than Jeremiah must have written it. Such a notion, however, is contrary to Jewish tradition and opinion. Even though the book itself makes no mention of the name of its author, there is no good reason not to ascribe it to the weeping prophet.

The book closes on a note of hope, with a prayer to the unchanging God to somehow bring about a spiritual revival of his people (see 5:19; 5:21). This same spiritual revival is needed in this world today to bring as many people into the kingdom of our triune God - before it is too late.

Ezekiel

This book is written by the third "major prophet". Ezekiel, like Jeremiah, was a priest called by God as a prophet. He had been taken captive to Babylon by Nebuchadnezzar along with King Jehoiachin and 10,000 of the leaders and skilled craftsmen of Judah (see 2 Kings 24:8-17).

Ezekiel's entire ministry was in Babylon (except for occasional visions of the corruption in the temple back at Jerusalem). His story starts shortly before the final destruction of the city and the temple under Nebuchadnezzar's third and final invasion of Judah. His early prophecies warn of the coming destruction while his later chapters speak of the future restoration of Israel and the future millennial temple. Some of his central chapters deal with prophecies of judgment on other nations besides Judah. It is in connection with the prophecy against Tyre that one of the most important revelations of the fall of Satan was given (Ezk. 28:11-19).

Much of Ezekiel – like Jeremiah – consists of verbatim quotations from God himself. The introduction of the various quotations ("the word of the Lord came unto me saying" – or equivalent) occurs some 60 times in Ezekiel. Ezekiel was a younger contemporary of Jeremiah and may well have known him and been instructed by him before the exile. Both were priests who had the same deep dedication to God and His Word. Further, it should be noted that Ezekiel's direct ministry had been to the tribes of Judah and Benjamin in the southern kingdom (the ten tribes of the northern kingdom had been carried away into Assyria over a century before, after more than two centuries of deep apostasy), yet many of his prophecies envision the reunion of Judah and Israel (Ezk 34,36,37) and their restoration to the worship of the true God when our Messiah comes to establish his kingdom on earth. With Israel now restored to its homeland after almost 2000 years in exile these prophetic events may not be all that far off. I pray for its return every day.

Daniel

The book of Daniel contains some of the most fascinating stories and prophecies in all the Bible. For me this book is the most important prophetic book in the Bible outside of Revelation. The book opens as the best and the brightest of the youth from the captured Israel are taken into Babylon to be assimilated into their culture. They are to eat, worship, and think only what their captors demand. This is similar to the indoctrination happening within the school system of America today. Any evidence not fitting into naturalism is excluded from consideration by students. Four of these youth named Daniel, Hananiah, Mishael and Azariah were removed from Judah to Babylon by Nebuchadnezzar. They were placed into the court of Eunuchs and renamed them Belteshazzar, Shadrach, Meshach and Abednego.

The king found favor with Daniel especially after Daniel interpreted king

The Three Hebrews in the Fiery Furnace

Pieter Aertsen - c. 1552

Nebuchadnezzar's dream. This dream portrays nations as a statue with a head of gold; breast and arms of silver; belly and thighs of brass; legs of iron; and feet a mixture of iron and clay. I believe these are vast time periods of earth history and we are now in the time period of the feet with the ten "predominate nations" being the European Union. We are approaching the period of the anti-Christ very rapidly and the moral relativism which clouds the thinking of many in our country makes it an easy target for the coming deception.

Most Christians have heard of the miraculous rescue of Daniel from the lion's den and the miraculous intervention saving Shadrach, Meshach and Abednego from the fiery furnace. In both cases Godly men refuse to worship any other than the true God and put their lives on the line as testimony to their convictions. God honored such faith. This message should certainly give us courage not to fall down to the coming false God, called the "antichrist" later in scripture.

The book of Daniel and Revelation has been subject to more criticism and rejection by critics than any book of the Bible except Genesis. This is probably because Daniel contains the account of so many supernatural miracles and foretelling of future events. Naturalistic critics cannot tolerate the idea that God knows the future and this book contains many remarkable fulfilled prophecies. Critics who refuse to believe in God's ability to reveal events through his prophets have gone to great lengths to deny the traditional authorship. They have charged historical errors and linguistic inconsistencies, but the real reason they hate Daniel is its prophecies.

Daniel in the Lions' Den

Peter Paul Rubens - 1615

All supposed arguments attempting to discredit Daniel have been refuted. Its main historical "errors" were references to Belshazzar and Darius the Mede, who were unknown to secular history – until they finally were identified as real rulers in the annals of Babylon and Persia. Daniel's supposed linguistic problems have also been refuted by identification of foreign words in Daniel, which would have been obsolete at the late date critics would like to ascribe to Daniel.

Daniel was recognized as a great wise and righteous man of God by his contemporary prophet Ezekiel (Eze. 14:14, 20; 28:3). All the ancient authorities, both Jewish and true Christians, accepted that Daniel was the author. The question is conclusively settled, however, by the fact that Jesus himself attributed one of the books most important prophecies to "Daniel the prophet" (Ma 24:15). There is every reason, therefore, to accept the authenticity of the book Daniel. Its histories are valid histories and its prophecies are genuine prophecies, many of them fulfilled already and the others awaiting the closing days of the age when the Lord returns.

Daniel served as a high official in Babylon under several kings beginning with Nebuchadnezzar (Dan. 2:48-29), followed by Evil-Merodach, Negal-Sharezar, Labashi-Marduk (none of whom are mentioned in Daniel) then under Babonidus and Belshazzar, who were sons of Nabonidus and co-regent with him in Babylon, at the time of the fall of Babylon to Persia (Dan. 5:29-31). He then continued under Darius the Mede and finally under Cyrus of Persia (Dan. 6:28). All of this seems to have occupied a total of almost 70 years (Dan. 9:2).

This book was written in the first person, Daniel asserting several times that he was the author (Dan. 8:1; 9:2-3). A substantial part of the book, from Daniel 2:4-7:28, was written in Aramaic, presumably because that was the court language in Babylon and because those portions of his book dealt mostly with events centering in the gentile kingdoms of the world, as distinct from those portions focusing especially on the nation of Israel and therefore written in Hebrew, among Hebrew portions is the great prophecy of the coming Messiah commonly known as "Daniel's 70 weeks" (Dan. 9:24-27). This amazing passage of Scripture gives an exact, to the day prediction for the appearance of the coming messiah followed by a prediction of the timing of significant climactic events coming at the end of the age. The language surrounding the last of the seventy weeks (the last 7 years of history) is yet to be fulfilled whereas the first 69 seven-year periods ended on the exact day Christ rode into Jerusalem on Psalm Sunday claiming to be God.

We now end the four Major Prophets and go next into the twelve books of the so-called Minor Prophets. However, no prophet is minor - all have been elected by our triune God to convey unto us, God's children, what we are to expect prior to our calling into heaven.

Hosea

Hosea is the first in the list of the Minor Prophets, so-called, mainly because their inspired books are shorter than those of the Major Prophets. Hosea probably was not the first of these prophets chronologically. More likely Amos, Obadiah, or Jonah were first. Hosea evidently was placed first among the Minor Prophets because his book was the longest of these. Hosea had occasionally been called "the brokenhearted prophet," because

The Prophet Hosea

James Tissot - ca. 1888

of the sad experiences in his own personal life, just as Jeremiah has been called "the weeping prophet."

The name Hosea means, "Jehovah is salvation." Hosea was unique among the prophets because he lived in the northern kingdom of Israel yet directed his prophecy against the southern kingdom of Israel. He warned against the coming Assyrian invasion of Israel - just as Jeremiah later warned Judah about Babylon. His prophecies concerning Israel were all during the 41 year reign of Jereboam II in Israel (Hosea 1:1; 2Kings 14:23). Hosea was also concerned about Judah and mentioned that his ministry coincided with the reigns of Uzziah, Jotham, Ahaz, and Hezekiah in Judah.

Some think that Hosea resided in Judah in his later years when opposition to his messages arose in Israel.

Hosea's prophecy centers on the divine inspired parallel between Hosea's love for his unfaithful wife and Jehovah's love for unfaithful Israel. In connection with his prophecies concerning Israel, a number of remarkable fulfillments in the long-range experiences of Israel (Hosea 3:4-5) have been fulfilled, verifing the supernatural nature of these prophecies.

Joel

Joel means "Jehovah is God". He was a prophet in Judah, probably one of the earliest of Judah's writing prophets. However, the date of his prophecy is uncertain, since there are no contemporary kings or other chronological data given. Nothing is known about Joel personally except that he probably lived in Jerusalem and that his father's name was Pethuel (Joel 1:1). This book is believed to be one of the earliest of the Minor Prophets because of the lack of condemnation of sin. Furthermore, the book contains no warning of impending invasion by either Assyria or Babylonia and no mention of the northern kingdom of Israel.

On the other hand, Joel speaks much of the coming "day of the Lord" (Joel 1:5) and God's judgment on the nations, looking far ahead to the end times. A recent devastating plague of locusts was taken by Joel as model for end time judgments. One significant confirmation of Joel's authorship of the book is the fact that the apostle Peter used a portion of it in his sermon on the day of Pentecost, attributing it to Joel (Acts 2:16-21 - citing Joel 2:28-32). Peter made note in this great sermon that a significant prophecy had been fulfilled in the pouring out of the Holy Spirit upon the early church.

Amos

Amos lived in Judah but he was greatly concerned about Israel's increasing departure from the true faith in Jehovah. Amos directed his prophecy mostly against this northern kingdom. He was a contemporary of Hosea, probably somewhat older. Amos makes a special point of the fact that he had been merely a shepherd, rather than a priest or trained prophet when God called him to the prophetic ministry (Amos 7:14-16). His prophecies centered on divine judgments on various other nations (Syria, Philistia, Tyre, Edom, Ammon, and Moab) before turning his attention to the sins of Judah and Israel. His judgments included both Israel and Judah, " the whole family"(Amos 3:1). However his predictions of future events were directed primarily at the northern kingdom with

Amos predicting that Israel was destined for captivity in Assyria (Amos 5:7; 6:9; 7:17).

Despite the imminent judgments, Amos closes on a great note of hope and assurance, promising the ultimate restoration of all the children of Israel in the Davidic kingdom - a prophecy James cites in the New Testament (Acts 15:15-18).

Obadiah

Obadiah means "servant of God". Obadiah was presumably a prophet of Judah, although this is not absolutely certain, there are several other men named Obadiah in the Bible, but none of them are the same as the author of the book. This one chapter prophecy of Obadiah is almost like a summary of the Old Testament. There is no clear evidence, either internal or external concerning the date of writing. Most conservative scholars believe that it is one of the earliest, perhaps the very first, of the prophetic books. Others, especially liberals who deny supernatural events such as telling of the future in advance, attribute its writing to the period after the destruction of Jerusalem.

The main theme of the book is a pronouncement of coming judgment on Edom (the nation descended from Esau - Jacob's brother). Though closely related to the Israelites, the Edomites were almost perpetually at enmity with them, even participating with another (unnamed) nation in an invasion and destruction of Jerusalem (see verses 11-15). There is no mention of the Babylonians in this situation, so it is possible that the reference is to a much earlier invasion of Jerusalem by the Edomites (see 2 Chron. 28:17) in the days of Ahaz. In any case, the ultimate doom of Edom is pronounced in view of both her arrogant pride (see verses 3-4) and also because her "violence against thy brother Jacob "(see verse 10). The complete judgment on Edom was long in coming, but eventually Edom and her Edomites disappeared from history, whereas Israel has continued to exist as a distinct people group right up to modern times. This itself is a minor miracle testifying to the hand of God upon the Jewish people.

My Christian brother John McTernan based his book, As America has done to Israel, upon the prophet Obadiah. I highly recommend this book because it documents why the U.S.A. has experienced so many catastrophes when it has opposed Israel or the Jewish people in its diplomatic relations. There is a strong case that how people treat Israel has a direct correlation to their long term prosperity.

Jonah

Jonah means "dove". According to Bible scoffers and liberal theologians this book is a big fish tale. I used to discuss the truth of God's word with the pastor that married Vivian and I. In discussing Jonah he said, "If some members of the church said they do not believe this part of the Bible, should I kick them out of the church?" I responded, "Of course not, your duty is to be so sincere and convincing when teaching God's Word as the truth, that there would be no doubt in anyone's mind".

Jonah is undoubtedly the most familiar of the Minor Prophets, because of the famous story of Jonah and the great fish. This factual account involves such a unique miracle that Jonah is the object of more skepticism than any other prophet except Daniel. Nevertheless, the book has been fully accepted as canonical and historical by both Jews and Christians – until modern times.

Even Jesus referred to the event as a real factual event and tied that fact to the reality of his resurrection (Matt. 12:40). Christ accepted the reality of Jonah's miraculous experience in the great fish, even making it a prophetic type of his own coming death and resurrection. Jesus pointed to the three days and three nights which Jonah spend inside the fish, essentially dead to the world, as a foreshadowing of his coming death for three days and three nights followed by his resurrection. Finally, the people accepted the almost equally amazing miracle of the repentance of Nineveh under Jonah's preaching (see Matt 12:41; Luke 11:29-30, 32). What more assurance could a Christian ask for in reality of this event than the testimony of it from the very mouth of Jesus?

Jonah was a prophet of Israel, rather early in the line of writing prophets. His home was in Gath-sepher, in Galilee, in the land of Zebulum, and he was identified as a real prophet in

Israel, during the reign of Jeroboam II (see 2 Kings 14:23, 25). There is thus no warrant for considering him merely a fictional character in a legendary tale, as many modern scholars have assumed.

In connection with Nineveh's repentance, it should be emphasized that Nineveh was the great capital of Assyria, the empire that would later invade Israel and carry its people off into captivity. The Assyrians had the reputation of being the most cruel and vicious people of any great nations of antiquity. A nationwide repentance, under the preaching of an Israelite prophet, was an absolutely amazing phenomenon. Yet its

Johan Leaving the Whale

Jan Brueghel the Elder - ca. 1600

authenticity is confirmed not only by Jonah but by Christ himself. One of the great lessons of the book of Jonah is that no matter how long or to what extent a culture rejects the Lord, His desire is to bring people back into fellowship and no-one is without hope. Evolution has been used in a might way to draw our youth away from trusting God or the Bible but there is still hope for returning America to the truth, one person at a time.

This national conversion lasted only about one generation or so, for Assyria and Nineveh later incurred God's wrath for their wickedness, and the prophet Nahum eventually pronounced their coming destruction (see Nahum 3:1, 7). It is striking to note that, with most of the pre-exilic prophets ministering in Israel and Judah, only this divinely directed ministry of Jonah was to a nation outside of Israel. Although Israel is God's chosen nation, he has never abandoned his concern for all nations, even a nation like Assyria.

Micah

Micah means "who is like Jehovah". Micah was a prophet from southwestern Judah, whose prophecy nevertheless dealt also with the northern kingdom, Israel, and its capital in Samaria. He was a contemporary of Isaiah and included some of the same prophecies (compare Mic. 4:1-3 and Isaiah 2:2-4). In fact, in his younger days Micah may have been a disciple of Isaiah.

He wrote his prophecy while Israel was still in the land, but only shortly before the Assyrian invasion and destruction of Israel (Mic. 1:1-6). There are indications in later chapters that he continued his ministry in Judah after seeing the fulfillment of Samaria's destruction. He also prophesied the eventual captivity of Judah (Mic. 4:10) - though this prophecy would not be fulfilled until over a century later. It is noteworthy that Jeremiah, the last prophet of Judah before the exile, quotes Micah's prophecy some 120 years later (Jer. 26:18 citing 3:12). According to Jeremiah, this prophecy was made at the time good king Hezekiah reined in Jerusalem.

Micah preached against wickedness of both Israel and Judah, yet he also prophesied the ultimate victory of God and his people through the coming Messiah. His book includes the wonderful prediction of our Messiah's human birth in Bethlehem, a prophecy which was specifically fulfilled over 700 years later. He predicted the eternal deity of our Messiah (Mic. 5:2), the rejection of our Messiah's first visitation of planet earth, and his second return when all remaining doubters will accept him on bended knee (Mic. 5:3). This book is a treasure of messages pointing directly toward Jesus.

Nahum

The name Nahum means "comfort" and his very name must have given comfort to the nation of Judah as he predicted the imminent destruction of her inveterate enemy, the unspeakable Assyrians, with their mighty capital, ancient Nineveh. Nahum is called an "Elkoshite", but the location of Elkosh is unknown. Many think that Elkosh was later renamed Kaphar Nahum ("the village of Nahum") in his honor. This city became Capernaum in the New Testament times and was a focal point of Jesus' travels. If so, Nahum was a native of the northern kingdom of Israel, but moved to Judah after the Assyrian invasion and destruction of Israel.

The entire prophecy is an indictment of Nineveh and speaks of its soon-coming judgment. Although it is not mentioned by Nahum, it had been about 150 years since the time of Jonah when Nineveh's king (and all the people) had repented of their wickedness and turned to the Lord. Sadly, six generations later Nineveh and the Assyrians had returned to all-consuming cruelty and evil. God makes it apparent through Nahum that he will not tolerate such sinfulness. He used Assyria to punish Israel, but now Assyria's time had come, and Nahum's prophecy announced it in no uncertain terms.

Some have suggested that Nahum prophesied during the reign of Hezekiah in Judah, but the evidence seems to fit better to the closing days of Josiah's rule. In any case, Nahum's prophecies against Nineveh were completely fulfilled.

Habakkuk

The book of Habakkuk indicates an author of deep spirituality and great concern for the holiness of God. In his third chapter, during an eloquent poetic prayer expressing great faith in the ultimate vindication of God's righteousness, he calls himself "Habakkuk the prophet". This is one of only two cases (Hag. 1:1 is the other example) where one of the Canonical prophets identify themselves specifically as a prophet of God. This is somewhat of a dangerous assertion because the test for a true prophet of God is 100% accuracy in the foretelling of future events. If anyone claims to be a prophet of God and is wrong even one time – the consequence is an instant death penalty.

Little is known about Habakkuk personally. He was evidently a contemporary of Jeremiah, in the closing years of Judah's partial independence before the Babylonian exile. His ministry was probably in the turbulent years just following good king Josiah's death and he clearly predicted the imminent Babylonian invasion and captivity (Hab. 1:5-11).

It is in Habakkuk that the famous assurance first appears that "the just shall live by his faith" (Hab. 2:4). This verse was quoted three times in the New Testament and eventually became the focal point of the protestant reformation under Martin Luther. It was the realization that we could do nothing to earn our salvation, and our actions add nothing to our righteousness before the Lord, that transformed Martin Luther's life (and eventually the Western world). It is only by accepting what Jesus has done upon our behalf that we become righteous before God. The heresy that we can obey some set of rules and thereby become good enough to earn our way back into favor with the Lord is again widely prevalent through the Western world today. And each denomination seems to have its own set of favorite rules. It is sad how we have permitted Satan to divide us into various denominations - leading Christians into splintered groups. Jesus, in one of his final pleas to God, stated that the world "would know us by our love" and prayed for the unity of believers. The very constitution of America acknowledges that "We the people…are one nation under God" yet this too has come to be forgotten and denied. Let us again return our focus to faith in God, what He has done for us, and his inerrant Word. In the same way I pray we will also as a country return to the clear understanding of the Constitution of the United States rather than twisting it to fit whatever we want it to mean.

Zephaniah

Zephaniah's name means "Jehovah has treasured". Zephaniah was Judah's descendant and the great-great grandson of one of the good kings of Judah - Hezekiah (see 1:1). He presumably lived and prophesied in Jerusalem. The book of Zephaniah contains dark pictures of impending doom on Judah but also points to bright glimpses of a future under the reign of the messiah. It is a beautifully written study - it contrasts both severe warnings and glorious promises.

Zephaniah himself prophesied during the reign of Josiah making him a contemporary of Jeremiah. It seems likely that his warnings may have contributed to the revival that took place under Josiah. During his later years Zephaniah foretold specifically of imminent judgments on other nations that were even more wicked – including Philistia (Zep. 2:4-7), Moab and Ammon (Zep. 2:8-22), Ethiopha (Zep. 2:12), and especially Assyria (Zep. 2:13-15). But God never leaves us hopeless and this book closes with a wonderful prophecy concerning the future messianic kingdom. At this future time all nations will serve the Lord and restored Israel will finally be, "A name and a praise among all people of the earth" (Zep. 3:20). I believe the current generation will live to see the fruition of this promise.

Haggai

Haggal was the first of the three post exile prophets, the others being his contemporaries, Zechariah, followed by Malachi. Haggai was called by God to rebuke and then encourage the Jews in connection with their divine commission to rebuild the temple. These circumstances are outlined in more detail in the books of Ezra and Nehemiah. Little is known of Haggai personally except that he identified himself as a prophet some five times (Hag. 1:1,3,12; 2:1,10). He was the only one of the prophets to do so except for Habakkuk (see Hab. 1:1). His ministry lasted only a few months, but was successful in motivating the people to work on the temple. Note references to his ministry in Ezra 5:1 and 6:14.

There are five books in the Bible with only one chapter and seven with three chapters but Haggai is the only book with two chapters. It is possible that Haggai was very old when he wrote this prophecy and may have been one of the very few Jews who had seen the original temple in all its glory fortunate enough to have returned to Jerusalem from exile (see Hag. 2:3; Ez. 3:12-13). This would account for both the urgency of his message and the brevity of his ministry.

Zachariah

Zachariah means "Jehovah remembers". He was both a priest and a prophet, being a grandson of another prophet, Iddo, and a member of the original company that had come to Jerusalem with the governor Zerubbabel (see 1:11 Neh. 12:4, 16). It is interesting that some 28 other Zachariahs are mentioned in the Old Testament, but this Zachariah is mentioned elsewhere only in Ezra 5:1 and 6:14, where Ezra confirms that both Haggai and Zachariah were instrumental in getting the discouraged Jews back to the job of building the temple.

The Lord blessed my daughter Virginia (Ginny) and Gregory Brockelsby with a son whom they named Zachary Shane. He was born on April 6, 1980 (3 months premature) at 2 lbs. 10 oz. The Lord called him back very shortly after his birth but before he did, he was used by our country's wonderful medical staff in a study to help keep alive other premature babies. The Lord has a way to bring good from the most terrible loss. My son-in-law told me Zachary's short life helped others and helped to ease the pain of his loss. So in his short lifetime God used him for a special purpose.

Zachariah's book is the longest and most important of the three post exile prophecies. The other post exile books are Haggai and Malachi. There are more messianic prophecies in Zachariah than in any of the other minor prophets. Zachariah began his prophetic ministry very soon after Haggai (compare Zach. 1:1 with Hag. 1:1). Both prophets urged the people to resume their lagging temple rebuilding project. In contrast to

The Angel Appears to Zechariah

Domenico Ghirlandaio - fresco 1486-1490

Haggai's brief ministry, the ministry of Zachariah continued for several decades. Some critics have argued that a "second

Zachariah" was author of the last six chapters of the book, but there is no historical basis for such a notion. Both divisions of the book are quoted in the New Testament with no suggestion of different sources. The subject matter of chapters 1-8 is quite different from that of chapters 9-14, making this the likely explanation for any differences in style and vocabulary. It is also probably that Zachariah wrote the second section at a much later time in his life.

The first six chapters of the book are largely occupied with ten remarkable visions, all apparently occurring on the same night. These visions and their symbolic figures relate somewhat to the current situation in Jerusalem but are more likely references to the distance future. Zachariah 7-8 records special messages from the Lord through Zachariah to the Jewish people, their priests, and their leaders.

Zachariah 9-14 is largely messianic dealing with both the first and second comings of Christ. Christ's first coming was only accepted at first by twelve devout Jews, but there is a worldwide gathering of messianic Jews today who acknowledge that Jesus is the Messiah. At the Lord's second coming "every knee shall bow and every tongue confess" that He is indeed the Lord. I believe this will happen in the very near future, so always be prepared. These chapters also deal with God's judgments on the nations and their eventual unification under the leadership of Israel in the messianic kingdom.

Malachi

The name "Malachi" means "my messenger", or possibly "my angel" (the Hebrew word for angel is Malak). The book of Malachi is the last book of the Old Testament. After Malachi there was some 400 "silent years" before Christ was born. Even after the birth of Christ it is estimated that another 50 or so years passed before the Gospels and other divinely inspired New Testament books (possibly James or Galatians) were written. Thus Malachi occupies a key place in the canon of Scripture with approximately 450 years passing before additional revelations from God were permanently penned.

Since nothing is known of Malachi personally, some commentators have suggested that Malachi wrote his prophecy shortly before Ezra came to Jerusalem, and thus that he came earlier than either Haggai or Zechariah. This conjecture is unwarranted. It is clear that the temple was complete and its regular worship long established by the time Malachi had come to rebuke its corruption by unfaithful priests and people (see 1:7; 2:8; 3:10). It is possible that he was prophesying around 430 B.C.

Malachi was a man thoroughly devoted to God and his righteousness, the last of the Old Testament prophets. He rebukes the same sins as did Nehemiah (compare 2:11; 3:8-10 with Neh. 13:23-31; 13:10-14). Malachi possibly wrote in the interim between the two periods of Nehemiah's stay and governing in Jerusalem. It is appropriate that Malachi, the last Old Testament prophet, should prophesy in Malachi 3:1 concerning the coming of John the Baptist (widely considered the first New Testament prophet). The last chapter of the last book of the Old Testament begins with, "Surely The Day is coming; it will burn like a furnace. All the arrogant and every evildoer will be stubble and That Day which is coming will set them on fire." and ends with, "He will turn the hearts of fathers to their children and the hearts of children to their fathers…". The Old Testament starts with a statement of God's unbelievable power and majesty, "In the beginning God created the heavens and the earth", and ends with statements revealing the Creator's holy Justice and the unfathomable Love. What a fitting end to the written revelation in the Old Testament.

conclusions

In my first book, ***By His Word: A Wake Up Call to America's Churches***, I covered the seven C's of history - namely Creation, Corruption, Catastrophe, Confusion, Christ, Cross, and the Consummation (still to come). This book left an enormous time gap between the Confusion of languages (and dispersion of people across the world) and the coming of Christ. This is the gap covered by the majority of the Old Testament revealing how our triune God worked throughout human history to show all people his love and his holy character. I have tried within this very brief book to summaries just a few highlights of this history - revealing how we are a "stiff-necked" people (as God stated), tending to only call on God when we are in trouble. Throughout time our loving God often gave us what we wanted, just as he is doing it today. Yet His ultimate desire is for our utmost "want" to be in fellowship with Him.

God is delaying his second coming while working through true Christians, to help bring people to return to a loving relationship with Him. Our job is to plant the seed of truth in fertile hearts and He will do the rest. Our Lord Jesus Christ was sent to show and demonstrate how humans made in his image should live in relationship to both God and each other. Jesus demonstrated what a loving father we have, willing to sacrifice his son, in an excruciating painful death, so we can gain everlasting life in their eternal kingdom through this sacrifice. By accepting Christ as our Lord and Savior, we can walk with God on a daily basis. What a wonderful gift our triune God has given us and it only requires our personal repentance and acceptance. *"Praise our Lord."*

Jesus Christ is the Son of God, Chief Cornerstone, the Beginning and End, the Anointed One, the Morning Star, Emmanuel (which means God is with us), the Lamb who takes away the sin of mankind, and the greatest prophet of all. He came to prepare his followers to be able to read the signs of these end times. Jesus pointed out that, in the midst of world upheaval, it is necessary to understand the meaning of key developments. Speaking to his disciples, Jesus described the events that would signal the final countdown to the apocalypse. He wanted his followers to be prepared for his second coming at the end of the age.

In his own prophecy, Jesus referred to a revelation from Daniel's vision (see Matthew 24:15; Daniel 9:24-27). Daniel's words – repeated hundreds of years later by Jesus – serve as a crucial guide as we attempt to understand the signs of our times. Jesus walked the earth some five centuries after Daniel recorded his prophecies. But both Jesus and Daniel looked ahead through time to our generation as they described events that will lead to the final battle between God and Satan. Jesus' prophetic message in Matthew 24 had a recurring theme: **be prepared!** Read this section of Scripture and compare it to the world around us today.

Jesus was very careful to give us the information we need to understand the times we live in and to prepare our hearts for what lies ahead. He said we should look for certain prophetic developments as they unfold, and he called our attention to Daniels vision: *"when ye therefore see the abomination of desolation, spoken by Daniel the prophet, stand in the holy place, (whoso readeth, let him understand)"* (Mathew 24:15). By quoting Daniel's prophecy about the Antichrist defiling the rebuilt temple in Jerusalem, Jesus gave this Hebrew prophet his divine seal of approval. Jesus points to Daniel because he wants us to be spiritually prepared for the challenges that lie just ahead. His words will guide and enlighten us as we study his prophecies and learn to identify the events that will characterize the end of this age.[2]

[2] **Countdown to the Apocalypse**, Grant R. Jeffrey Pg's 11, 12

I have read end time revelations from Daniel and Revelation many times. I see these events as very close to taking place. I do not claim to be a prophet with special revelation from God, so take this scenario as just my best guess of what I see unfolding (based on Scriptural predictions and current events). Human knowledge seems to be doubling about every two years. IBM's "Blue Gene" supercomputer can complete one million billion calculations every second. All this seems to be a fulfillment of Daniel's prophecy that "knowledge will be increased". European Union is now becoming a major world force and will likely take control of our future - ultimately producing the "Antichrist". Someday soon a seven year peace agreement will take place which will permit Israel to rebuild their third temple. They already have everything in place to do this and are just waiting for the right opportunity to re-establish their ancient sacrificial practices. With the temple complete and Jewish sacrifices again taking place, the Antichrist will create the "abomination of desolation" by claiming to be God within the temple itself. He will be killed by a severe blow to his head at this mid-point of the tribulation and brought back to life by Satan. This major miracle to a world leader will solidify his power over most of the planet. This is the time I believe the rapture will take place (removing the major restraint to evil which individual Christians represent) and permitting Satan to control the world through the Antichrist. The Antichrist will declare himself to be God and most will believe, because of Satan's resurrection of the Antichrist back to life. This will bring all of the Judgments spoken of in Revelations. The purpose of these judgments will be to draw the last of the true believers to the one true God but this will be a horrible time of earth history. I thank God that those who have given their lives to the Lord prior to this time will not have to suffer God's judgments against the unbelieving world that remains.

Biblical Chronology

I believe that a true shepherd can be easily detected from a false shepherd by observing how they handle the Word of God. However, you must know this true Word before you can detect error! A pastor who teaches the straightforward understanding of God's Word is the clearest indication of a shepherd who has been called of the Lord vs. a man who is a pastor by vocation seeking to please the world. I have met with many shepherds and in my opinion many have chosen the role as a professional vocation rather than a calling from the Lord. There have been similar examples throughout history and our modern age. An example of both historical saints (called of God) and modern wolves (dressed as sheep) can be found in the contrast between Bishop James Ussher and modern evangelist Hugh Ross.

In *The Annals of the World* Bishop James Ussher used a vast number of ancient records and came to the conclusion that our planet was created by God on October, 23, 4004 B.C. Ussher devoted his life to the study of both God's Word and world history and was widely acknowledged as a scholarly and Godly man. Although this may not be the exact day or year that the earth was created, the vast majority of dating methods do indicate that the earth is much younger than the widely parroted "millions of years". The Bible clearly teaches that it is in the range of 6000 years old. An updated version of *The Annals of the World* have been compiled by Larry and Marion Pierce who did an excellent job of using Ussher's Latin notes and the 1658 English version. I highly recommend it as a tool for understanding how Biblical history connects with the history of what was happening on earth throughout time.

Hugh Ross is a representative of many Christian "leaders" who deny both a recent creation and worldwide flood (the two are intimately connected). They are actually false prophets. Somehow such compromising Christian teachers expect people to take the rest of the Bible seriously while undermining it at the beginning. This is totally illogical. If we cannot believe the Bible in a straightforward way at the beginning, at what verse do we need to accept what it clearly states... vs. twisting God's Word to make it say what we want to believe? The ultimate result of denying the accuracy of God's Word at the very beginning is driving people away from the Bible and Christianity seriously.

Playing to a largely evolution-believing audience, Ross recently placed a "dunce-hat" in a cartoon of James Ussher in order to promote his old-earth, evolution promoting compromises. Many of our modern day theologians have accepted Hugh Ross' version of earth's history (rather than Ussher's) resulting in widespread confusion as to what the Bible actually teaches. Yet an unbiased, straightforward reading of God's Word should result in the acknowledgment of a real, recent, literal creation (which explains biological life) and a globe covering flood (which explains geology and the fossil record). Although the Bible is neither biology nor a geology textbook, these real events provide an unchanging and unerring foundation for understanding both scientific disciplines in a way which fits scientific observation and has stood the test of time. Hugh Ross is misleading thousands and disparaging sincere brilliant scholars of the past in order to promote his convoluted, Bible-undermining teachings.

I will conclude by summarizing what God has done throughout history with a list of people through whom he has worked - citing these people as instruments of God indwelled with his Holy Spirit. Their names deserve to be mentioned and honored. You will notice how this recounting of history is intertwined with the people Satan (Lucifer) used to try to destroy God's plan of redemption for planet earth.

In eternity past, there has always been God the father, God the son, and the energizing Holy Spirit, *"from everlasting to everlasting, thou art our triune God."* (Psalm 90:2). God created angels as companions, but lead by Lucifer (the rebellious one), one third of these spiritual beings rebelled against God and were cast from his presence (out of heaven into the unseen spiritual realm on earth). Our God of love sought loving companions and next created Adam and Eve in his image. These two disobeyed God by eating the forbidden fruit (knowledge of good and evil) thereby allowing Lucifer's spirit to influence God's originally perfect human race. This evil influence continues to this day and can only be resisted by those whose spirit has been regenerated - by accepting the sacrifice of Christ on their behalf and thus becoming again worthy of being indwelled by God's Holy Spirit. From this first human couple came Cain, Abel, Seth and other children. Cain yielded next to Satan's temptations and became the first murderer. After Seth, came Enos, Cainan, Mahalaleel, Jared, Enoch, Methuselah, Lamech and Noah.

The earth was so filled with violence at this point in time that God destroyed it and only Shem, Ham and Japheth along with their wives (plus Noah and his wife) survived this world-wide deluge. The family line leading to Jesus went through Arphaxad, Caninan, Shelah, Eber, Peleg, Reu, Serug, and Nahor. In the process came Babel and the table of nations, splitting the human race into various cultural and ethnic groups via linguistic barriers. The language barrier caused various religious barriers among these groups yet every culture has a remembrance of the great world wide flood.

God decided he would use one man to promote truth into his confused world. He chose Terah's son Abram (later named Abraham). Satan's spirit strongly influenced Ishmael while the Holy Spirit worked to bring a savior to humanity thru Isaac. Then came the twins, with Satan's spirit continuing through Esau and the Holy Spirit continued to guide Jacob. Each time God chose one line of humanity ultimately leading to the Savior, it was opposed by another line of humanity seeking to destroy it. The spiritual battle between light and darkness could not be more apparent. God was with Jacob in spite of his many flaws and continued his work to redeem the world through him (God later changed Jacob's name to Israel).

From Jacob came the twelve sons, Ruben, Simeon, Levi, Judah, Dan, Naphtali, Gad, Asher, Issachar, Zebulun, Joseph and Benjamin. Joseph was the one who brought all these tribes to Egypt. They were enslaved in Egypt 400 years. Next came Moses, Aaron and Joshua - bringing the great historical accounts of God's mighty hand working through the Passover, the Exodus from Egypt, the worship within the Tabernacle and finally the Israelites being lead into the Promised Land.

Following the takeover of the Promised Land by God's chosen people came the years of leadership by the judges of Israel (for approximately 400 years). There were Othniel, Ehud, Shamgar, Deborah, Gideon, Abimelech (also a rebel king), Tola, Jair, Jephthah, Ibzan, Elon, Abdon and Sampson. Not being satisfied with judges, the people demanded a king. God gave his people what they wanted even though he knew problems would result.

In the united Israel the kings were Saul, David and Solomon. Evil abounded and the country was split into two kingdoms - Judah and Israel. The kings of Judah were Rehoboam, Abijah, Asa, Jehoshaphat, Jehoran, Ahaziah, Athaliah, Joash, Amaziah, Uzziah, Jotham, Ahaz, Hezekiah, Manasseh, Amon, Josiah, Jehoahaz, Jehoiakim, Jehoiachin and Zedekiah. The kings of Israel were Jeroboami, Nadab, Baasha, Elah, Zimri, Tibni, Omri, Ahab, Ahaziah, Jehoram, Jehu, Johoahaz, Jehoash, Jeroboam II, Zechariah, Shallum, Menahem, Pekahiah, Pekah and Hoshea.

During the reign of kings there were also prophets of God. God used these men to speak words of truth, warning, comfort, and prophecy to the nation of Israel (and the entire world). The Major Prophets were Isaiah (700 B.C.), Jeremiah (600 B.C.), Ezekiel and Daniel. The Minor Prophets were Hosea, Joel, Amos, Obadiah, Jonah, Micah, Nahum, Habakkuk, Zephaniah, Haggai, Zechariah and Malachi. As predicted by the prophets Israel was judged for its idolatry and the people led into captivity approximately 722 B.C. Judah was captured including the city of Jerusalem approximately 586 B.C. God's people were in exile approximately 70 years before their return from captivity. The rebuilding of the temple was competed approximately 515 B.C.

While all of this was going on the family line leading from David to Jesus was developing. These names are as follows: David, Solomon, Rehoboam, Abijah, Asa, Jehoshaphat, Joram, Uzziah, Jotham, Ahaz, Hezekiah, Manasseh, Amon, Josiah, Jezoniah, Shealtiel, Zerubbabel, Abiud, Eliakim, Azor, Zadok, Achim, Eliud, Eleazar, Matthan, Jacob and Joseph.

Yet Joseph is just the legal father of the Lord linking him to the throne of David. Jesus was born of a virgin and had no earthly father. As a matter of fact, the people of Israel became so rebellious and wicked under the leadership of one of their kings that it was prophesized that the savior could not come through the line of David…yet other prophetic statements stated the savior had to come through the line of David. How could this be? By making David's earthly father only his legal adoptive father, yet making his earthly mother a blood relative! The line from David to Mary is as follows: David, Nathan, Mattatha, Menna, Melea, Eliakim, Jonam, Joseph, Judah, Simeon, Levi, Matthat, Jorim, Eliezer, Joshua, Er, Elmadam, Cosam, Addi, Melchi, Neri, Shealtiel, Zerubbabel, Rhesa, Joanan, Joda, Joseph, Semein, Mattathias, Maath, Naggai, Hesli, Nahum, Amos, Mattathias, Joseph, Jannai, Melchi, Levi, Matthat, Eli, Mary, and Jesus. Thus the lineage from David to both Joseph and Mary come through David (one by blood and one through legality). With the birth of our Lord and Savior, all of God's promises to mankind are fulfilled.

There is a period of 400 years, from the end of the Old Testament to the start of the New Testament, with no record of God dealing with his people, thus this time is called the "silent years." We do not have any recorded history of our Lord after his birth until he is approximately 12 years old (as recorded in Luke). Later yet the Gospels take up the narrative with the New Testament prophet John the Baptist proclaiming Jesus Christ as the son of God.

Early in his ministry the Lord selected the following men to be his disciples: Peter, Andrew, James, John, Philip, Bartholomew, Thomas, Matthew, James, Thaddeus, Simon and Judas. None where selected for their renown, wealth, or abilities… but because they were willing to follow the Lord in faith. The closest disciples of the Lord were the same number as the tribes of Israel. He taught them to bring God's message to all the world. One of them had the spirit of Satan (Judas) and was used in one final attempt to destroy the redeemer of mankind. Yet God (who foreknows all things) saw this in advance and used the evil of Satan as the very vehicle by which he would bring forgiveness to a rebellious humanity. Judas was later replaced by Matthias. Jesus knew the hearts of all of these men. That is why they were selected to establish his kingdom here on earth. ***Are you one of those selected?*** You will only know if you become willing to repent of your sins, accept the sacrifice of Christ on your behalf, and find yourself filled with the desire to serve him.

My son Tim and I have chosen one of Paul's statements of faith to end this book - Galatians 2:20. *"I have been crucified with Christ; it is no longer I who live, but Christ who lives in me; and the life which I now live in the flesh, I live by faith in the son of God, who loved me and gave himself for me."*

Thank you Lord Jesus, for selecting someone as unworthy as I to proclaim your love to others.

- John Filippi

Other Resources

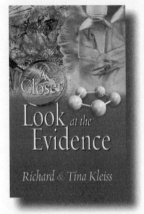

A Closer Look at the Evidence is another one-of-a-kind book from Search for the Truth Publications. Organized in 26 different scientific areas, each page ties together God's Word with God's world. Great for use as a daily devotional! Softcover, 414 pg, $5^{1/2}$ x $8^{1/2}$

Censored Science: The Suppressed Evidence is the most graphically stunning book we have ever offered. Every page is both a visual masterpiece in full color and intellectually mind opening. Learn what is being left out of student textbooks. Written in an understandable and fascinating way! Softcover, 112 pg, $8^{1/2}$ x 11

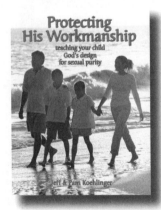

Protecting His Workmanship provides help for the parent child "sex-talk". This interactive and thoroughly biblical study is a wonderful resource for equipping teens to stay sexually pure in our sex-saturated society. Softcover workbook, 112 pg, $8^{1/2}$ x 11

SEE ALL OUR RESOURCES
AT WWW.SEARCHFORTHETRUTH.NET

Search for the Truth Publications

Mail-In Order Form

E-MAIL, SEND, OR CALL:

SEARCH FOR THE TRUTH MINISTRIES
TRUTH@SEARCHFORTHETRUTH.NET
3275 MONROE RD.
MIDLAND, MI 48642
989.837.5546

	Price per book			
	Single	**2-9**	**10+**	**Case Price**
God's Chosen People	9.95	5.95	4.00	Call
A Closer Look at the Evidence	11.95	8.95	6.00	Call
Censored Science	14.95	11.95	7.50	Call
Protecting God's Workmanship	11.95	8.95	6.00	Call

Resource	Quan.	Cost Each	Total
God's Chosen People			
A Closer Look at the Evidence			
Censored Science			
Protecting God's Workmanship			

Ship Order To

NAME:

ADDRESS:

CITY/ST/ZIP:

PHONE:

Subtotal	
MI residents add 6% sales tax	
Shipping : add 15% of subtotal	
TOTAL ENCLOSED	

- Please make checks payable to "Search for the Truth Ministries"
- Normal delivery time is 1-2 weeks
- For express delivery, increase shipping to 20% of order